T0059099

DIE WALKÜRE

Music Drama in Three Acts

(From the trilogy DER RING DES NIBELUNGEN)

by

Richard Wagner

**English Version by
STEWART ROBB**

Ed. 2565

G. SCHIRMER, Inc.

45612c

DIE WALKÜRE

Richard Wagner was born in Leipzig, Germany, on May 22, 1813. A poor student at school, he grew absorbed in music, which he learned from private teachers. His first attempt at opera, *Die Hochzeit*, was written before his twentieth birthday. *Die Feen*, never to be staged in his lifetime, was completed in 1834. Two years later, *Das Liebesverbot*, based on Shakespeare's *Measure for Measure*, was given at the Magdeburg Opera, where Wagner served as conductor; the work proved a failure and spelled bankruptcy for the company. After a stint as conductor in Riga, he went to Paris; there he was inspired by the example of Giacomo Meyerbeer, whose influences on *Rienzi* (1840) are marked.

The following year Wagner wrote *Der fliegende Holländer*, the first work in which his musical individuality emerged. The two operas that followed, *Tannhäuser* (1845) and *Lohengrin* (1850), further developed his concept of a modern stage form in which music, words, gesture and scenery would blend as never before. All the while his fame grew, amid stormy public and personal battles. The composition of *Der Ring des Nibelungen*, of which *Die Walküre* is the second music drama, saw Wagner casting aside all remnants of romantic grand opera. He selected a legendary subject that could be adapted without regard for precedent. The roots of the *Ring* lie in the Scandinavian *Edda* and a corresponding German saga, the *Nibelungenlied*, on which Wagner had begun research as early as the 1840's. The *Ring*'s text was written in reverse order, *Götterdämmerung*, *Siegfried*, *Die Walküre*, *Das Rheingold*. The music, however, was composed in the order of performance, bringing gradual fruition of Wagner's thought through amplification of the more than eighty themes which interlace his musical fabric.

It took the composer two decades to complete the *Ring*. *Die Walküre*, written one year after *Das Rheingold*, kept him busy through the winter of 1854 and spring of 1855. The most popular of the Ring dramas, it brought Wagner to a white heat of inspiration, especially the first act, in which the tragic figures of Siegmund and Sieglinde won his special sympathy. The character of Fricka, it is said, represents Wagner's feelings about the bonds of conventional marriage, made unbearable to him by his first wife, Minna. Ironically enough, *Die Walküre's* great popularity has all but undermined Wagner's plan to have the *Ring* always played in its entirety and to have audiences follow its lofty, abstract ideas as a whole.

In addition to the music dramas already mentioned, Wagner composed *Tristan und Isolde* (1859), *Die Meistersinger von Nürnberg* (a comedy, 1867) and *Parsifal* (1882). The upheavals that rocked the composer's life were in part cushioned by the generous sponsorship of Ludwig, the King of Bavaria, and his marriage to Cosima Liszt. Wagner died on February 13, 1883, while on vacation in Venice. His memorial remains the Festspielhaus in Bayreuth, a vast theater Wagner had built to his own specifications in 1876. To this day his works are presented there during July and August.

The world premiere of *Die Walküre* took place at the Hof-und-National Theater in Munich on June 26, 1870. The work reached America seven years later, April 2, 1877, when it was performed at the New York Academy of Music. The Metropolitan Opera added *Die Walküre* to its repertory, during the company's second season, on January 30, 1885; on that occasion the conductor was Leopold Damrosch and the Brünnhilde a singer of Bayreuth fame, Amalia Materna.

THE STORY

ACT I. At the height of a raging storm, Siegmund the Volsung falls exhausted into a deserted hut. Soon a young woman enters from another room; discovering the wounded man, she restores him with a draught of water. She tells him she is Sieglinde, wife of the chieftain Hunding. Mysteriously drawn to her, as she is to him, Siegmund exclaims that he must leave, lest he bring her misery, but Sieglinde pleads with him to stay awhile. Before long, heavy footsteps announce the approach of Hunding, who eyes his guest suspiciously but grants him a night's rest. At supper, Siegmund relates his story: named "Woeful," he has lost mother, sister and father. He is weaponless, having lost his sword defending a girl from being forced into marriage. Hunding rises angrily, proclaiming that it was his kin whom Siegmund defied. He warns that in the morning they must fight. Though Sieglinde tries to draw Siegmund's glance toward the great ash tree, she is thwarted by Hunding, who drives her within. Left alone, Siegmund calls on his father for the sword promised in his hour of need. Sieglinde returns to tell the youth how she was forced to marry Hunding and how, at their wedding feast, a one-eyed stranger had thrust a sword into the great ash tree. As the doors fly open and moonlight floods the hut, Siegmund declares his love; she hails him as the spring that follows winter's frost. Suddenly Sieglinde recognizes her wooer's face and voice as her own. When he cries out that his father was Volsa, she joyously bestows on her long-lost twin brother his true name — Siegmund. Naming the sword "Notung," Siegmund draws it from the tree: as Sieglinde falls on his breast, he bids her follow him as sister and bride. Unmindful of the consequences, the lovers flee.

ACT II. On a rocky mountain pass, Wotan orders the Valkyrie Brünnhilde, his warrior daughter born of Erda, to protect his mortal son Siegmund in the youth's coming battle with Hunding. No sooner has she promised to obey than Wotan is confronted by his wife Fricka, goddess of marriage. Fricka berates her husband for condoning a union between brother and sister, angrily denouncing him for abetting lawlessness that he has practiced himself. Wotan regretfully agrees not to aid Siegmund. As Fricka strides off in triumph, Brünnhilde returns and, consoling her father, draws from him the long history of the ring's curse. When his youthful ardor faded, he was sustained by the hope of recovering the ring from Fafner through his son's valor. He departs, warning Brünnhilde not to protect Siegmund. Night falls as the two lovers stagger in, pursued by Hunding's dogs; Sieglinde, begging Siegmund to leave her, sinks to the ground in exhaustion. As Siegmund rests beside her, Brünnhilde comes to announce his fate. Siegmund's refusal to be parted from Sieglinde moves the Valkyrie to promise help in spite of Wotan's orders. At the sound of Hunding's horn, Siegmund goes to seek battle, leaving Sieglinde to awaken deliriously. Brünnhilde shields the hero until Wotan appears, his spear pointed toward his son; Siegmund's sword shatters and he is felled by Hunding. While Wotan stands stunned by his son's death, Brünnhilde carries Sieglinde to safety. Waking to reality, Wotan makes a scornful gesture toward Hunding, who falls dead, and furiously goes off in search of Brünnhilde.

ACT III. On the Valkyries' rock, eight warlike maidens return from battle. Soon Brünnhilde rushes in with Sieglinde, begging her sisters to save the girl; the Valkyries refuse. Handing Siegmund's sword to Sieglinde, she hails her as the woman who will bear the world's mightiest hero, Siegfried. Sieglinde goes off to seek a forest refuge and Brünnhilde turns to face the wrath of the approaching Wotan. The Valkyries, at first hiding their sister, flee when they hear the fate Wotan decrees for Brünnhilde: she is to sleep on the Valkyries' rock, a helpless mortal, prey to the first man who finds her. Brünnhilde pleads her cause; was shielding Siegmund indeed a crime and not Wotan's true will? Relenting, Wotan lightens her punishment: flames encircling her resting place will protect her from any but a fearless hero. Overwhelmed by emotion, Wotan takes his beloved daughter in his arms and bids her farewell. Kissing her eyes closed, he leads her to the rock where she will sleep. Calling Loge, Wotan traces a circle of fire.

Courtesy Opera News

CAST OF CHARACTERS

SIEGMUND, Wotan's mortal son . . . . Tenor

SIEGLINDE, his sister . . . . Soprano

HUNDING, Sieglinde's husband . . . . Bass

WOTAN, king of the gods . . . . Baritone

BRÜNNHILDE, a Valkyrie, his daughter by Erda . . . . Soprano

FRICKA, queen of the gods . . . . Mezzo-Soprano

GERHILDE ⎫ . . . . Soprano

WALTRAUTE ⎪ . . . . Mezzo-Soprano

SCHWERTLEITE ⎪ . . . . Mezzo-Soprano

ORTLINDE ⎬ *Valkyries* . . . . Soprano

HELMWIGE ⎪ . . . . Soprano

SIEGRUNE ⎪ . . . . Mezzo-Soprano

ROSSWEISSE ⎪ . . . . Mezzo-Soprano

GRIMGERDE ⎭ . . . . Mezzo-Soprano

SYNOPSIS OF SCENES

DIE WALKÜRE

ACT ONE

The Interior of a Dwelling

In the center is the stem of a mighty ash tree, whose roots spread far over the ground. The tree is separated from its crown by a timber roof which is pierced to allow the spreading limbs to pass through. Round the trunk a room is built; the walls are of roughly-hewn logs, hung here and there with matting and woven hangings. To the right in the foreground is the fireplace, behind which is an inner room like a storeroom, approached by mounting a few steps and separated from the forepart of the hall by a plaited curtain, half thrown back. In the background an entrance door with a wooden latch. Farther in the front, but on the same side, there is a table and behind it a broad wooden bench fastened to the wall; a few wooden stools stand before the table.

Siegmund hastily opens the entrance door from without and enters. It is nearly evening; a violent thunderstorm is just subsiding. Siegmund holds the latch in his hand for a moment and scans the room. He looks exhausted, and his disordered garments indicate a fugitive. Perceiving no one he closes the door behind him, strides to the hearth and there throws himself down, exhausted, on a rug of bearskin.

SIEGMUND

No matter whose hearth,
here I must slumber.

(He sinks back and remains stretched out motionless a while. Sieglinde enters through the door of the inner chamber.)

SIEGLINDE

A stranger here!
I must accost him.
(She advances a few steps.)
Who is this man
that lies by the hearth?

(As he does not stir, she approaches still nearer and observes him.)

Really weary
and travel-worn!
Maybe unconscious too!
Could he be sick?
(She bends closer to him.)
His breath is still coming;
his eyes remain closed, though.
Brave and strong seems the man,
though he fell fatigued.

SIEGMUND

(suddenly lifting his head)
A drink! A drink!

SIEGLINDE

I'll fetch one for you.
(She quickly takes a drinking horn, leaves the house, returns with the horn filled, which she hands to Siegmund.)
Here's refreshment
for lips that are parching:
water, which you did want.

(Siegmund drinks and returns the horn. After a nod of thanks he regards her with increasing attention.)

SIEGMUND

Cooling refreshment
came from the spring:
my weight of woe
now is more light.
My courage returns.
My eye enjoys
the blessed pleasure of sight —
But who restores me to life?

SIEGLINDE

This house and this wife
belong to Hunding.
Let him welcome his guest:
stay till he comes back home!

SIEGMUND

Weaponless am I.
The wounded guest
cannot worry your husband.

SIEGLINDE

Oh, show your wounds right away!

1

DIE WALKÜRE

ERSTER AUFZUG
Das Innere eines Wohnraumes

In der Mitte steht der Stamm einer **mächtigen Esche, dessen Wurzeln** *sich weithin in den Erdboden verlieren; von seinem Wipfel ist der Baum durch ein gezimmertes Dach geschieden, welches so durchschnitten ist, dass der Stamm und die nach allen Seiten hin sich ausstreckenden Äste hindurchgehen. Um den Eschenstamm ist ein Saal gezimmert; die Wände sind aus roh behauenem Holzwerk; hier und da mit geflochtenen und gewebten Decken behangen. Rechts im Vordergrund steht der Herd; hinter dem Herd befindet sich ein innerer Raum, gleich einem Vorratsspeicher, zu dem man auf einigen hölzernen Stufen hinaufsteigt; davor hängt, halb zurückgeschlagen, eine geflochtene Decke.*

Als der Vorhang aufgeht, öffnet Siegmund von aussen hastig die Eingangstür und tritt ein: es ist gegen Abend, starkes Gewitter, im Begriff sich zu legen. Siegmund hält einen Augenblick den Riegel in der Hand und überblickt den Wohnraum: er scheint von übermässiger Anstrengung erschöpft; sein Gewand und Aussehen zeigen, dass er sich auf der Flucht befinde. Da er niemand gewahrt, schliesst er die Tür hinter sich, schreitet auf den Herd zu und wirft sich dort ermattet auf eine Decke von Bärenfell.

SIEGMUND
Wes Herd dies auch sei,
hier muss ich rasten.

(Er sinkt zurück und bleibt einige Zeit regungslos ausgestreckt. Sieglinde tritt aus der Tür des inneren Gemaches.)

SIEGLINDE
Ein fremder Mann?
Ihn muss ich fragen.
(Sie tritt ruhig einige Schritte näher.)
Wer kam ins Haus
und liegt dort am Herd?

(Da Siegmund sich nicht regt, tritt sie noch etwas näher und betrachtet ihn.)
Müde liegt er
von Weges Mühn:
schwanden die Sinne ihm?
Wäre er siech?
(Sie neigt sich zu ihm herab.)
Noch schwillt ihm der Atem;
das Auge nur schloss er.
Mutig dünkt mich der Mann,
sank er müd' auch hin.

SIEGMUND
(fährt jäh mit dem Haupt in die Höhe)
Ein Quell! Ein Quell!

SIEGLINDE
Erquickung schaff' ich.
(Sie nimmt schnell ein Trinkhorn, geht damit aus dem Haus, kommt zurück und reicht das gefüllte Trinkhorn Siegmund.)
Labung biet' ich
dem lechzenden Gaumen:
Wasser, wie du gewollt!
(Siegmund trinkt und reicht ihr das Horn zurück. Als er ihr mit dem Haupte Dank zuwinkt, haftet sein Blick mit steigender Teilnahme an ihren Mienen.)

SIEGMUND
Kühlende Labung
gab mir der Quell,
des Müden Last
machte er leicht;
erfrischt ist der Mut,
das Aug' erfreut
des Sehens selige Lust.
Wer ist's, der so mir es labt?

SIEGLINDE
Dies Haus und dies Weib
sind Hundings Eigen;
gastlich gönn' er dir Rast:
harre, bis heim er kehrt!

SIEGMUND
Waffenlos bin ich:
dem wunden Gast
wird dein Gatte nicht wehren.

SIEGLINDE
Die Wunden weise mir schnell!

1

SIEGMUND

(*shakes himself and springs up quickly to a sitting position*)

They're scratches, all.
There's nothing to see.
My limbs are still firmly
fixed in their frame.
Had my shield and spear been as good,
half as strong as my arm was,
never would I have fled.
But my spear and my shield are gone.
The hounds oppressed and
harried me hard,
and raging storms
spent all my strength.
Yet fast as I fled the hunters,
faster weariness went.
Night fell, with a rest to my eyes;
the sun now smiles in my face.

SIEGLINDE

(*has filled a horn with mead and extends it to him*)

I trust you will take this
mellow mead,
sweet in its creamy taste.

SIEGMUND

Will you not taste it first?

(*Sieglinde does so, then hands him the horn again. Siegmund takes a long draught, then returns the horn. For a long time the two remain silent, looking at each other with growing interest.*)

You have helped one who is Fortune's
foe.
May all evil
be turned from you.

(*He rises hastily as if about to leave.*)

I've rested sweetly,
and feel refreshed.
Now I'll go on my way.

SIEGLINDE

Who pursues you, that you must flee?

SIEGMUND

Misfortune hunts me
in all my fleeings.
Misfortune dogs me
in all my goings.
May all this keep from you far!
Now must I take my leave.

(*He goes to the door and lifts the latch.*)

SIEGLINDE

Stay here instead!
You bring no sorrow within,
where sorrow already dwells.

SIEGMUND

(*Deeply moved, he remains motionless and searches Sieglinde's features. Finally he returns and resumes his seat by the hearth.*)

Woe-king — that is my name,
so I'll wait here for Hunding.

(*Sieglinde remains in silence; then she starts and listens. Hunding is heard leading his horse to the stable outside. She hastens to open the door. Hunding enters, armed with shield and spear. In the doorway he stops on beholding Siegmund.*)

SIEGLINDE

(*meeting her husband's questioning look*)

Here he fell,
weary and worn.
Need brought him inside.

HUNDING

You tended him?

SIEGLINDE

I cooled his thirsty lips
as a hostess should.

SIEGMUND

Food and drink,
thanks to her.
Then will you call her guilty?

HUNDING

Holy is my hearth,
holy to you my house.

(*to Sieglinde, giving her his weapons*)

Bring the food for us men.

(*Sieglinde hongs the weapons on the tree, fetches food and drink from the storeroom and sets the table.*)

(*Hunding scans Siegmund's features sharply and compares them with those of his wife.*)

How strong the resemblance!
Through eyes like to hers
gleams the glittering serpent.

(*He turns with apparent unconcern to Siegmund.*)

Far indeed
must you have fared!
You rode no steed,
yet found this place.
What sorry pathway
led to your woe?

SIEGMUND

*(springt lebhaft vom Lager
zum Sitz auf)*

Gering sind sie,
der Rede nicht wert;
noch fügen des Leibes
Glieder sich fest.
Hätten halb so stark wie mein Arm
Schild und Speer mir gehalten,
nimmer floh ich dem Feind;
doch zerschellten mir Speer und Schild.
Der Feinde Meute
hetzte mich müd',
Gewitterbrunst
brach meinen Leib;
doch schneller, als ich der Meute,
schwand die Müdigkeit mir:
sank auf die Lider mir Nacht,
die Sonne lacht mir nun neu.

SIEGLINDE

*(füllt ein Horn mit Met und
reicht es Siegmund)*

Des seimigen Metes
süssen Trank
mögst du mir nicht verschmähn.

SIEGMUND

Schmecktest du mir ihn zu?

*(Sieglinde nippt am Horn und reicht
es ihm wieder. Siegmund tut einen
langen Zug, indem er den Blick mit
wachsender Wärme auf sie heftet. Er
seufzt tief auf und senkt den Blick
düster zu Boden. Mit bebender
Stimme.)*

Einen Unseligen labtest du:
Unheil wende
der Wunsch von dir!

*(Er bricht schnell auf, um
fortzugehen.)*

Gerastet hab' ich
und süss geruht:
weiter wend ich den Schritt.

SIEGLINDE

Wer verfolgt dich, dass du schon
fliehst?

SIEGMUND

Misswende folgt mir,
wohin ich fliehe;
Misswende naht mir,
wo ich mich zeige.
Dir, Frau, doch bleibe sie fern!
Fort wend' ich Fuss und Blick.

*(Er schreitet bis zur Tür und hebt den
Riegel.)*

SIEGLINDE

So bleibe hier!
Nicht bringst du Unheil dahin,
wo Unheil im Hause wohnt!

*(Siegmund bleibt tief erschüttert stehen
und forscht in Sieglindes Mienen;
diese schlägt verschämt und traurig
die Augen nieder. Langes Schweig-
en.)*

SIEGMUND

(kehrt zurück)

Wehwalt hiess ich mich selbst:
Hunding will ich erwarten.

*(Sieglinde fährt plötzlich auf, lauscht
und hört Hunding, der sein Ross
aussen zum Stall führt. Sie geht
hastig zur Tür und öffnet; Hunding,
gewaffnet mit Schild und Speer, tritt
ein und hält unter der Tür, als er
Siegmund gewahrt.)*

SIEGLINDE

(dem Blicke Hundings entgegnend)

Müd' am Herd
fand ich den Mann:
Not führt' ihn ins Haus.

HUNDING

Du labtest ihn?

SIEGLINDE

Den Gaumen letzt' ich ihm,
gastlich sorgt' ich sein!

SIEGMUND

Dach und Trank
dank ich ihr:
willst du dein Weib drum schelten?

HUNDING *(zu Sieglinde)*

Heilig ist mein Herd:
Heilig sei dir mein Haus!

*(Er legt seine Waffen ab und übergibt
sie Sieglinde.)*

Rüst' uns Männern das Mahl!

*(Sieglinde hängt die Waffen an Ästen
des Eschenstammes auf, dann holt
sie Speise und Trank aus dem Spei-
cher und rüstet auf dem Tische das
Nachtmahl.)*

*(Hunding misst scharf und verwundert
Siegmunds Züge, die er mit denen
seiner Frau vergleicht.)*

Wie gleicht er dem Weibe!
Der gleissende Wurm
glänzt auch ihm aus dem Auge.

*(Er wendet sich wie unbefangen zu
Siegmund.)*

Weit her, traun,
kamst du des Weg's;
ein Ross nicht ritt,
der Rast hier fand:
welch schlimme Pfade
schufen dir Pein?

SIEGMUND

Through wood and meadow,
thicket and heath,
storm drove me forth,
and pressing need.
I know not the way that I came.
Nor do I better
know where I've come to.
This is now what I would learn.

HUNDING

(at the table, beckoning Siegmund to
a seat)
The roof above,
the house around —
these are Hunding's own.
If you go west
when you leave this place
you'll reach my kin
in their rich homesteads.
They guard the honor of Hunding.
May I ask of my guest
to inform me now of his name?
(Siegmund remains thoughtfully silent.
Sieglinde, seated beside Hunding, op-
posite Siegmund, fixes her eyes on
the latter.)

HUNDING

Should you fear to
show me your trust,
my wife here likes to listen.
See, she hangs upon your words!

SIEGLINDE

Guest, I would learn
who you are.

SIEGMUND

"Peaceful" no one should name me;
"Joyful" — would that I were!
Just let me call myself "Woe-king"!
Wolfe — he was my father.
I came one of a pair.
We were twins, my sister and I.
Both did I lose,
mother and maid,
she who gave birth,
and my partner in birth.
Short was the time they were mine.
Wolfe was strong and stalwart,
but foes were many and fierce.
The father fared
to the hunt with the youngster.
One time we returned
all tired from the hunt,
and found our lair laid waste.
Our lordly hall
was ruined by fire,
our oak once blooming,

now was a stump.
My mother lay murdered,
brave-hearted soul!
All trace of my sister
was lost in wrack.
The Neidings' cruel band
were cause of this bitter deed.
My father fled,
an outcast with me.
Years and years the
youngster did live with
his father within the wild.
Many hunts
were made for the two,
but still the wolf-pair
withstood their foes.
(to Hunding)
A Wolfing tells you of this,
whom as Wolfing many well know.

HUNDING

Wild and amazing stories
certainly, doughty guest,
Woe-king — the Wolfing!
I think I have heard of this pair,
through dark and evil rumors.
Wolf though, or Wolfing
I've never known.

SIEGLINDE

But tell me further, stranger,
where dwells your father now?

SIEGMUND

A mighty outcry was raised.
Neidings were hot on our heels.
But many hunters
fell to the Wolfings,
in flight through the woods
slain by their game!
Our foe was scattered like chaff.
My father, though, vanished just then,
and he left no traces
though long I did seek him.
And a wolfskin was all
that I ever found.
Then my wish, shunning the woods,
now drew me to menfolk and women.
The ones I found,
no matter where,
though friends to know,
or maids to woo,
always gave scorn to the outcast.
Evil lay on me.
Whatever I thought right
others looked on as wrong.
What looked evil to me
others favored as right!
No matter where I went

SIEGMUND

Durch Wald und Wiese,
Heide und Hain,
jagte mich Sturm
und starke Not:
nicht kenn ich den Weg, den ich kam.
Wohin ich irrte,
weiss ich noch minder:
Kunde gewänn' ich des gern.

HUNDING
(am Tisch und Siegmund den
Sitz bietend)

Des' Dach dich deckt,
des' Haus dich hegt,
Hunding heisst der Wirt;
wendest von hier du
nach West den Schritt,
in Höfen reich
hausen dort Sippen,
die Hundings Ehre behüten.
Gönnt mir Ehre mein Gast,
wird sein Name nun mir genannt.
(Siegmund blickt nachdenklich vor sich
hin. Sieglinde, die sich neben Hunding, Siegmund gegenüber, gesetzt,
heftet ihr Auge auf diesen.)

HUNDING

Trägst du Sorge,
mir zu vertraun,
der Frau hier gib doch Kunde:
sieh, wie gierig sie dich frägt!

SIEGLINDE

Gast, wer du bist,
wüsst' ich gern.

SIEGMUND

Friedmund darf ich nicht heissen;
Frohwalt möcht ich wohl sein:
doch Wehwalt muss ich mich nennen.
Wolfe, der war mein Vater;
zu zwei kam ich zur Welt,
eine Zwillingsschwester und ich.
Früh schwanden mir
Mutter und Maid;
die mich gebar
und die mit mir sie barg,
kaum hab ich je sie gekannt.
Wehrlich und stark war Wolfe;
der Feinde wuchsen ihm viel.
Zum Jagen zog
mit dem Jungen der Alte:
von Hetze und Harst
einst kehrten sie heim:
da lag das Wolfsnest leer.
Zu Schutt gebrannt
der prangende Saal,
zum Stumpf der Eiche
blühender Stamm;

erschlagen der Mutter
mutiger Leib,
verschwunden in Gluten
der Schwester Spur.
Uns schuf die herbe Not
der Neidinge harte Schar.
Geächtet floh
der Alte mit mir;
lange Jahre
lebte der Junge
mit Wolfe im wilden Wald:
manche Jagd
ward auf sie gemacht;
doch mutig wehrte
das Wolfspaar sich.
(zu Hunding gewandt)
Ein Wölfing kündet dir das,
den als "Wölfing" mancher wohl kennt.

HUNDING

Wunder und wilde Märe
kündest du, kühner Gast,
Wehwalt, der Wölfing!
Mich dünkt, von dem wehrlichen Paar
vernahm ich dunkle Sage,
kannt' ich auch Wolfe
und Wölfing nicht.

SIEGLINDE

Doch weiter künde, Fremder:
wo weilt dein Vater jetzt?

SIEGMUND

Ein starkes Jagen auf uns
stellten die Neidinge an:
der Jäger viele
fielen den Wölfen,
in Flucht durch den Wald
trieb sie das Wild:
wie Spreu zerstob uns der Feind.
Doch ward ich vom Vater versprengt;
seine Spur verlor ich,
je länger ich forschte:
eines Wolfes Fell nur
traf ich im Forst;
leer lag das vor mir,
den Vater fand ich nicht.
Aus dem Wald trieb es mich fort;
mich drängt' es zu Männern und
  Frauen.
Wieviel ich traf,
wo ich sie fand,
ob ich um Freund',
um Frauen warb,
immer doch war ich geächtet:
Unheil lag auf mir.
Was Rechtes je ich riet,
andern dünkte es arg,
was schlimm immer mir schien,
andere gaben ihm Gunst.
In Fehde fiel ich, wo ich mich fand,

there was strife.
Wrath found me,
go where I would.
When I sought pleasure
Sorrow was found.
And so I am rightly "Woe-king,"
for sorrow only is mine.

HUNDING

With so sad a lot as your share,
the Norns are not your friends.
No one greets you with joy
to whom you come as guest.

SIEGLINDE

Only cowards would fear
a weaponless, lonely man.
Tell me yet, guest,
how in the strife
you lost your weapon at last.

SIEGMUND (*more animatedly*)

A child in distress
called for my help.
Her kinsmen wanted
to marry the maiden
to one whom her heart could not love.
Straightway I went,
eager to aid.
I gave the gang
trouble to spare.
The victor felled the foes.
Struck down in death lay the brothers.
The maiden clung fast to her slain.
Her wrath gave place to her grief.
She poured forth floods of tears.
She wailed the hardness of fate.
At the loss of the slaughtered brothers
loud were the cries of the bride.
Then the slain men's kinsmen
stormed to the place,
overwhelming,
eager to venge themselves.
Foemen came raging,
circling the homestead.
Yet would the maid
cling to her dead.
My spear and shield
guarded her long,
till spear and shield
were hewn from my grip.
Standing weaponless, wounded,
I beheld the bride die,
while warriors were pressing me hard.
On the corpses she lay dead.
(*looking at Sieglinde with pained
fervor*)
You know now, questioning wife,
why my name cannot be "Peaceful."

(*He gets up and steps over to the
hearth. Sieglinde casts down her eyes,
deeply moved.*)

HUNDING (*very darkly*)

I know a riotous race:
it does not revere
what others do.
It's hated by all, and by me.
I heard the summons to vengeance,
payment demanded
for blood of kin.
I came too late,
went back to my home,
and found the cursed tracks
within my very own house.
Just now, Wolfing,
you are secure.
For this night you are my guest.
But arm yourself with
strong weapons tomorrow:
that day is chosen for strife.
You'll pay me what the deed pays.
(*to Sieglinde, who has anxiously step-
ped between the two men*)
Out of the room!
Loiter not here!
Prepare my drink for the night,
and wait for me within.
(*Pensively, Sieglinde takes a drinking
horn from the table, goes to a cup-
board from which she takes spices,
and turns toward the chamber. On
reaching the uppermost step near the
door she again turns her head toward
Siegmund, who stands calmly and
sullenly by the hearth, never losing
sight of her. She casts at him a long
and significant glance, by which she
endeavors to direct his attention to
a spot in the ash tree. Hunding,
noticing the delay, warns her off with
a commanding look. She disappears
through the door with the torch and
drinking horn.*)

HUNDING

(*taking his weapons from the tree*)
A man has need of his arms.
I'll see you, Wolfing, with morning.
You heard what I said —
guard yourself well!
(*He goes into the chamber with his
arms.*)
(*Night has fallen. The hall is dimly
lit by the dying fire. Siegmund sinks
down on the bench by the fire and
reflects with some perturbation.*)

Zorn traf mich, wohin ich zog;
gehrt' ich nach Wonne,
weckt' ich nur Weh:
drum musst' ich mich Wehwalt
　　nennen;
des Wehes waltet' ich nur.

HUNDING

Die so leidig Los dir beschied,
nicht liebte dich die Norn:
froh nicht grüsst dich der Mann,
dem fremd als Gast du nahst.

SIEGLINDE

Feige nur fürchten den,
der waffenlos einsam fährt!
Künde noch, Gast,
wie du im Kampf
zuletzt die Waffe verlorst!

SIEGMUND (immer lebhafter)

Ein trauriges Kind
rief mich zum Trutz:
vermählen wollte
der Magen Sippe
dem Mann ohne Minne die Maid.
Wider den Zwang
zog ich zum Schutz,
der Dränger Tross
traf ich im Kampf:
dem Sieger sank der Feind.
Erschlagen lagen die Brüder:
die Leichen umschlang da die Maid,
den Grimm verjagt' ihr der Gram.
Mit wilder Tränen Flut
betroff sie weinend die Wal:
um des Mordes der eignen Brüder
klagte die unsel'ge Braut.
Der Erschlagnen Sippen
stürmten daher;
übermächtig
ächzten nach Rache sie;
rings um die Stätte
ragten mir Feinde.
Doch von der Wal
wich nicht die Maid;
mit Schild und Speer
schirmt' ich sie lang,
bis Speer und Schild
im Harst mir zerhaun.
Wund und waffenlos stand ich —
sterben sah ich die Maid:
mich hetzte das wütende Heer —
auf den Leichen lag sie tot.
(mit einem Blick voll schmerzlichen
　　Feuers auf Sieglinde)
Nun weisst du, fragende Frau,
warum ich Friedmund — nicht heisse!

(Er steht auf und schreitet auf den
　Herd zu. Sieglinde blickt tief er-
　schüttert zu Boden.)
　　　HUNDING (sehr finster)
Ich weiss ein wildes Geschlecht,
nicht heilig ist ihm,
was andern hehr:
verhasst ist es allen und mir.
Zur Rache ward ich gerufen,
Sühne zu nehmen
für Sippenblut:
zu spät kam ich
und kehre nun heim,
des flücht'gen Frevlers Spur
im eignen Haus zu erspähn.
Mein Haus hütet,
Wölfing, dich heut';
für die Nacht nahm ich dich auf;
mit starker Waffe
doch wehre dich morgen;
zum Kampfe kies ich den Tag:
für Tote zahlst du mir Zoll.
(Sieglinde schreitet mit besorgter Ge-
　bärde zwischen die beiden Männer
　vor.)
Fort aus dem Saal!
Säume hier nicht!
Den Nachttrunk rüste mir drin
und harre mein zur Ruh'.
(Sieglinde, mit ruhigem Entschluss
　öffnet den Schrein, füllt ein Trink-
　horn und schüttet aus einer Büchse
　Würze hinein. Dann wendet sie das
　Auge auf Siegmund, um seinem
　Blick zu begegnen, den dieser fort-
　während auf sie heftet. Auf den
　Stufen kehrt sie sich noch einmal um,
　heftet das Auge sehnsuchtsvoll auf
　Siegmund und deutet mit dem Blick
　andauernd und mit sprechender
　Bestimmtheit auf eine Stelle am
　Eschenstamme. Hunding fährt auf
　und treibt sie mit einer heftigen
　Gebärde zum Fortgehen an.)
　　　HUNDING
Mit Waffen wahrt sich der Mann.
Dich, Wölfing, treffe ich morgen;
mein Wort hörtest du —
hüte dich wohl!
(Er geht mit den Waffen in das
　Gemach.)

(Es ist vollständig Nacht geworden; der
　Saal ist nur noch von einem schwach-
　en Feuer im Herd erhellt. Siegmund
　lässt sich, nah' beim Feuer, auf dem
　Lager nieder und brütet in grosser
　innerer Aufregung eine Zeitlang vor
　sich hin.)

SIEGMUND

I'd find a sword, said my father,
in time of my greatest need.
Swordless I came here,
my host a foe.
As his vengeance' pledge
here do I stand.
A wife hailed me,
noble and fair.
A lovely anguish
burns my heart.
The woman for whom I long,
she whose magic casts a sweet spell,
is held in thrall by the man
who scorns one who's unarmed.
Volsa, Volsa,
where is your sword,
that mighty sword
I can swing in battle?
Does there now break from my breast
what raged in my heart till now?

(*The fire falls together. From the
aroused glow a bright ray strikes that
spot of the ash tree trunk Sieglinde
had indicated where a buried sword
hilt is now revealed.*)

What glistens there
in glimmering light?
From the ash stem
I perceive a gleam.
Unseeing eyes are
lit by its look.
See, it laughs in my face.
How my heart takes fire
to see it shine.
Is it the glance
the glorious wife
left behind her
to cling to the tree
as she went out the hall?

(*The fire on the hearth is beginning to
die out.*)

Deepening darkness
shadowed my eyes,
but the glance she shed
brightened my gloom,
bringing me daylight and warmth.
Sweet the sunlight
appeared to me.
It scattered around me
its radiant glance,
till mountains hid it from view.
Yet once more ere it set
came the blessing again.
And the ancient ash's stem
was lit by the golden glow.
The flush has faded.

The light grows dim.
Gathering darkness
weighs on my eyelids.
Deep in my quiet bosom
gleams an invisible flame.

(*The fire has quite gone out. It is deep
night. The chamber door opens softly. Sieglinde, in a white robe, enters
and approaches Siegmund.*)

SIEGLINDE

Sleeping, guest?

SIEGMUND

(*springing up with joyful surprise*)
Who steals this way?

SIEGLINDE

It's I, listen to me!
In heavy sleep lies Hunding.
I mingled a drug with his drink.
Use up the night to your good!

SIEGMUND (*interrupting*)
Good comes when you're near!

SIEGLINDE

Let me guide you now to a weapon.
Oh might you win this sword!
I then might call you
noblest of heroes.
The strongest alone
bears off the prize.
Oh, mark it well, all that I tell you!
The band of kinsmen
sat here in hall,
invited as guests to his wedding.
He courted a maid
whom, quite unasked,
villains had brought him for bride.
Sad I sat there,
while they were drinking.
A stranger entered the hall,
an old man, suited in gray.
Pulled down was his hat
so one of his eyes was hidden.
Yet the other's glare
put all in terror.
All the guests felt
its threatening force.
I alone
felt from its power
sweet, longing distress,
comfort and tears combined.
On me looking,
he scowled at the others,
as he swung a sword in his hands,
then drove it deep
in the ash's stem,

SIEGMUND

Ein Schwert verhiess mir der Vater,
ich fänd' es in höchster Not.
Waffenlos fiel ich
in Feindes Haus;
seiner Rache Pfand,
raste ich hier,
Ein Weib sah ich,
wonnig und hehr:
entzückend' Bangen
zehrt mein Herz.
Zu der mich nun Sehnsucht zieht,
die mit süssem Zauber mich sehrt,
im Zwange hält sie der Mann,
der mich Wehrlosen höhnt!
Wälse! Wälse!
Wo ist dein Schwert?
Das starke Schwert,
das im Sturm ich schwänge,
bricht mir hervor aus der Brust,
was wütend das Herz noch hegt?

(*Das Feuer bricht zusammen; es fällt
aus der aufsprühenden Glut plötzlich
ein greller Schein auf die Stelle des
Eschenstammes, welche Sieglindes
Blick bezeichnet hatte, und an der
man jetzt deutlich einen Schwertgriff
haften sieht.*)

Was gleisst dort hell
im Glimmerschein?
Welch ein Strahl bricht
aus der Esche Stamm?
Des Blinden Auge
leuchtet ein Blitz:
lustig lacht da der Blick.
Wie der Schein so hehr
das Herz mir sengt!
Ist es der Blick
der blühenden Frau,
den dort haftend
sie hinter sich liess,
als aus dem Saal sie schied?

(*Von hier an verglimmt das Herdfeuer
allmählich.*)

Nächtiges Dunkel
deckte mein Aug';
ihres Blickes Strahl
streifte mich da:
Wärme gewann ich und Tag.
Selig schien mir
der Sonne Licht;
den Scheitel umgliss mir
ihr wonniger Glanz,
bis hinter Bergen sie sank.
Noch einmal, da sie schied,
traf mich abends ihr Schein;
selbst der alten Esche Stamm
erglänzte in goldner Glut:

da bleicht die Blüte,
das Licht verlischt;
nächtiges Dunkel
deckt mir das Auge:
tief in des Busens Berge
glimmt nur noch lichtlose Glut.

(*Das Feuer ist gänzlich verloschen:
volle Nacht. Das Seitengemach öffnet
sich leise: Sieglinde, in weissem
Gewande, tritt auf den Herd zu.*)

SIEGLINDE

Schläfst du, Gast?

SIEGMUND

(*freudig überrascht aufspringend*)
Wer schleicht daher?

SIEGLINDE

Ich bin's: höre mich an!
In tiefem Schlaf liegt Hunding;
ich würzt' ihm betäubenden Trank:
nütze die Nacht dir zum Heil!

SIEGMUND (*unterbrechend*)
Heil macht mich dein Nah'n!

SIEGLINDE

Eine Waffe lass mich dir weisen:
O wenn du sie gewännst!
Den hehrsten Helden
dürft' ich dich heissen:
dem Stärksten allein
ward sie bestimmt.
O merke wohl, was ich dir melde!
Der Männer Sippe
sass hier im Saal,
von Hunding zur Hochzeit geladen.
Er freite ein Weib,
das ungefragt
Schächer ihm schenkten zur Frau.
Traurig sass ich,
während sie tranken;
ein Fremder trat da herein:
ein Greis in blauem Gewand;
tief hing ihm der Hut,
der deckt' ihm der Augen eines;
doch des andren Strahl,
Angst schuf er allen,
traf die Männer
sein mächt'ges Dräu'n:
mir allein
weckte das Auge
süss sehnenden Harm,
Tränen und Trost zugleich.
Auf mich blickt' er
und blitzte auf jene,
als ein Schwert in Händen er schwang;
das stiess er nun
in der Esche Stamm,

till it went up to the hilt.
There's one who can win the weapon:
he who can draw it out.
But all who tried it,
despite all their efforts,
at last were forced to give up.
Guests were coming,
and guests were going,
the strongest tugged at the steel—
but they could not budge it a bit.
The sword is resting there still.
I knew then who it was
that had greeted me in gloom.
I know too
who alone
must pull the sword from the tree.
Oh, if I could find
today, that friend,
come from afar
who would give me help.
The things I have suffered
in anguish of soul,
the pain I have felt
from scorn and from shame—
sweetest revenge would
pay for these sorrows!
I'd win back all
the good I had lost;
Indeed, I'd regain
all I had mourned for—
if I could find that dear friend
and clasp him firm in my arms!

SIEGMUND

(*embracing her ardently*)

O, radiant one,
I am that friend
who's heir both to sword and wife!
Hot in my breast
burns now the oath
which weds me, dear one, to you.
For all I have sought
I meet now in you.
In you, loved one,
I find what I've lacked.
Shame has been yours,
and woe has been mine.
Men have despised me,
and you have been scorned.
Joyful revenge now
smiles on the happy!
I laugh out
in holy delight,
clasping you close to my bosom,
feeling the throb of your heart.

SIEGLINDE

(*in alarm, tearing herself away*)

Oh, who's that? Who came just now?

(*The outer door has sprung wide open. Outside the night is beautiful. The full moon shines upon the two, and all about them suddenly becomes visible.*)

SIEGMUND

No one went—
yet someone came.
See now, the spring
laughs in the hall!
Storms of winter yield to
the joyful May.
The spring is shining:
mild is his light.
On gentle breezes,
light and lovely,
weaving patterns,
see him move.
Through wood and mead
his breath is stirring.
Widely open
laugh his eyes.
The blissful song of birdlings
shows his voice.
Gentle perfumes
scent his breath.
From his ardent blood are blooming
beautiful flowers.
Bud and sprout
up-spring at his word.
His gently wielded rod
holds sway over earth.
Winter and storm bow to
his potent rule.
So surely no door so strong
but must yield its might to his power.
That obstinate door
once—kept us from him.
To greet his sister
swiftly he flew.
Fond love attracted the spring.
Within our bosoms,
deep it lay hid,
but now it laughs in the light.
The bride who is sister
is freed by the brother.
What kept them apart
lies broken to bits.
Joyous greetings unite the pair,
and love and spring are made one.

SIEGLINDE

You are the spring,
the spring I have longed for
in time of the winter frost.

bis zum Heft haftet' es drin:
dem sollte der Stahl geziemen,
der aus dem Stamm es zög'.
Der Männer alle,
so kühn sie sich mühten,
die Wehr sich keiner gewann;
Gäste kamen
und Gäste gingen,
die stärksten zogen am Stahl —
keinen Zoll entwich er dem Stamm:
dort haftet schweigend das Schwert.
Da wusst' ich, wer der war,
der mich Gramvolle gegrüsst;
ich weiss auch,
wem allein
im Stamm das Schwert er bestimmt.
O fänd' ich ihn heut'
und hier, den Freund;
käm' er aus Fremden
zur ärmsten Frau:
was je ich gelitten
in grimmigem Leid,
was je mich geschmerzt
in Schande und Schmach —
süsseste Rache
sühnte dann alles!
Erjagt hätt' ich,
was je ich verlor,
was je ich beweint,
wär' mir gewonnen,
fänd' ich den heiligen Freund,
umfing' den Helden mein Arm!

SIEGMUND
(*mit Glut Sieglinde umfassend*)
Dich, selige Frau,
hält nun der Freund,
dem Waffe und Weib bestimmt!
Heiss in der Brust
brennt mir der Eid,
der mich dir Edlen vermählt.
Was je ich ersehnt,
ersah ich in dir;
in dir fand ich,
was je mir gefehlt!
Littest du Schmach,
und schmerzte mich Leid;
war ich geächtet,
und warst du entehrt:
freudige Rache
ruft nun den Frohen!
Auf lach' ich
in heiliger Lust —
halt ich die Hehre umfangen,
fühl ich dein schlagendes Herz!

SIEGLINDE
(*fährt erschrocken zusammen und
reisst sich los*)

Ha, wer ging? Wer kam herein?

(*Die Tür springt auf: aussen herrliche
Frühlingsnacht; der Vollmond leuchtet herein und wirft sein helles Licht
auf das Paar.*)

SIEGMUND
Keiner ging,
doch einer kam:
siehe, der Lenz
lacht in den Saal!
Winterstürme wichen
dem Wonnemond,
in mildem Lichte
leuchtet der Lenz;
auf lauen Lüften
lind und lieblich,
Wunder webend
er sich wiegt;
durch Wald und Auen
weht sein Atem,
weit geöffnet
lacht sein Aug'.
Aus sel'ger Vöglein Sange
süss er tönt,
holde Düfte
haucht er aus:
seinem warmen Blut entblühen
wonnige Blumen,
Keim und Spross
entspringt seiner Kraft.
Mit zarter Waffen Zier
bezwingt er die Welt;
Winter und Sturm wichen
der starken Wehr:
wohl musste den tapfern Streichen
die strenge Türe auch weichen,
die trotzig und starr
uns — trennte von ihm.
Zu seiner Schwester
schwang er sich her;
die Liebe lockte den Lenz:
in unsrem Busen
barg sie sich tief;
nun lacht sie selig dem Licht.
Die bräutliche Schwester
befreite der Bruder;
zertrümmert liegt,
was je sie getrennt;
jauchzend grüsst sich
das junge Paar:
vereint sind Liebe und Lenz!

SIEGLINDE
Du bist der Lenz,
nach dem ich verlangte
in frostigem Winters Frist.

My heart gave you hail
with holiest awe
when at first your glance shone upon
  me.
All I had looked on was strange.
All that was near me was friendless,
as though all things that I met
had not ever been known.
But you, though, I
thoroughly knew.
And I knew you were mine
when I first saw you.
What was hid in my heart,
what I am,
broke on my mind,
clear as the day,
as cymbals of brass
break on the ear,
when within this frosty bleakness
at last I beheld my friend.
(*She hangs upon his neck in rapture
  and looks into his face.*)

SIEGMUND

O, sweetest of raptures!
Woman most blest!

SIEGLINDE

Oh, let me clasp you
and hold you near me,
that I may look on
the holy light
that from your eyes
and countenance shines,
and so sweetly masters my sense!

SIEGMUND

The moon of spring
shines on you bright;
how attractive
your wavy hair.
At last I know
what captured my heart:
I joy in feasting my gaze.

SIEGLINDE

How wide and open
gleams your brow.
Your temple displays
all the interlaced veins.
I tremble and my captive
holds me entranced.
A wonder takes my attention:
Before this first time we met
my eyes had seen your face!

SIEGMUND

I too recall
a dream of love:
an ardent longing
brought me your sight!

SIEGLINDE

A brook I looked in
gave back my face—
and now again I behold it:
what once the pool did reveal
now is reflected by you!

SIEGMUND

You are the picture
long hid in my heart!

SIEGLINDE
(*quickly turning aside her gaze*)

Oh, still! That voice!
Just let me listen!
I heard, as a child,
similar sounds.
Yet no! I heard them just lately,
when from the woods there came
the echoing peal of my voice.

SIEGMUND

What ravishing lute tones
capture my hearing!

SIEGLINDE
(*again gazing into his eyes*)

I've already seen
the glow of these eyes—
The stranger in gray
glanced at me thus,
and he thereby dispelled my woe.
By his look
his child knew the truth
and almost could give him his name.
(*She pauses, then resumes softly.*)
Are you "Woe-king" indeed?

SIEGMUND

Don't call me so.
Since you are mine,
I'm lord now of highest rapture!

SIEGLINDE

And could you joy to
take the name "Peaceful"?

SIEGMUND

Give me the name
that you'd love men to call me:
I'll take the name that you give!

SIEGLINDE

And yet you called Wolfe your father?

SIEGMUND

A wolf to the coward foxes!
This one, whose eyes
lightened as proudly
radiant one,
as yours do now,
was called—Volsa by name.

Dich grüsste mein Herz
mit heiligem Grau'n,
als dein Blick zuerst mir erblühte.
Fremdes nur sah ich von je,
freundlos war mir das Nahe;
als hätt' ich nie es gekannt
war, was immer mir kam.
Doch dich kannt' ich
deutlich und klar:
als mein Auge dich sah,
warst du mein Eigen;
was im Busen ich barg,
was ich bin,
hell wie der Tag
taucht' es mir auf,
wie tönender Schall
schlug's an mein Ohr,
als in frostig öder Fremde
zuerst ich den Freund ersah.

(*Sie hängt sich entzückt an seinen Hals
und blickt ihm nahe ins Gesicht.*)

SIEGMUND

O süsseste Wonne!
Seligstes Weib!

SIEGLINDE

O lass in Nähe
zu dir mich neigen,
dass hell ich schaue
den hehren Schein,
der dir aus Aug'
und Antlitz bricht
und so süss die Sinne mir zwingt.

SIEGMUND

Im Lenzesmond
leuchtest du hell;
hehr umwebt dich
das Wellenhaar:
was mich berückt,
errat ich nun leicht —
denn wonnig weidet mein Blick.

SIEGLINDE

Wie dir die Stirn
so offen steht,
der Adern Geäst
in den Schläfen sich schlingt!
Mir zagt es vor der Wonne,
die mich entzückt!
Ein Wunder will mich gemahnen:
den heut' zuerst ich erschaut,
mein Auge sah dich schon!

SIEGMUND

Ein Minnetraum
gemahnt auch mich:
in heissem Sehnen
sah ich dich schon!

SIEGLINDE

Im Bach erblickt' ich
mein eigen Bild —
und jetzt gewahr ich es wieder:
wie einst dem Teich es enttaucht,
bietest mein Bild mir nun du!

SIEGMUND

Du bist das Bild,
das in mir ich barg.

SIEGLINDE

(*den Blick schnell abwendend*)

O still! Lass mich
der Stimme lauschen:
mich dünkt, ihren Klang
hört' ich als Kind —
Doch nein! ich hörte sie neulich,
als meiner Stimme Schall
mir widerhallte der Wald.

SIEGMUND

O lieblichste Laute,
denen ich lausche!

SIEGLINDE

(*ihm wieder in die Augen spähend*)

Deines Auges Glut
erglänzte mir schon:
so blickte der Greis
grüssend auf mich,
als der Traurigen Trost er gab.
An dem Blick
erkannt' ihn sein Kind —
schon wollt' ich beim Namen ihn
    nennen!

(*Sie hält inne und fährt dann leise
    fort.*)

Wehwalt heisst du fürwahr?

SIEGMUND

Nicht heiss' ich so,
seit du mich liebst:
nun walt ich der hehrsten Wonnen!

SIEGLINDE

Und Friedmund darfst du
froh dich nicht nennen?

SIEGMUND

Nenne mich du,
wie du liebst, dass ich heisse:
den Namen nehm' ich von dir!

SIEGLINDE

Doch nanntest du Wolfe den Vater?

SIEGMUND

Ein Wolf war er feigen Füchsen!
Doch dem so stolz
strahlte das Auge,
wie, Herrliche, hehr dir es strahlt,
der war: — Wälse genannt.

SIEGLINDE

(beside herself)

Was Volsa your father,
and are you a Volsung?
Then it's for you—
his sword in the tree!
So let me then call you,
as I do love you,
Siegmund.
I'll call you that.

SIEGMUND

(springing over to the tree and seizing
fast the sword)

Siegmund say I,
and Siegmund am I:
bear witness this sword
I grip without shrinking!
Volsa made promise
in greatest need
this would be mine.
I hold it now!
Love that's most holy,
greatest need,
love with its longing,
need with desire,
brightly burn in my breast,
urging deeds and death!
Notung! Notung!
let that be your name—
Notung! Notung!
Sword that I need!
Show me your sharp
and cutting tooth.
Come out of the scabbard to me!

(With mighty tug he draws the sword
from the tree and shows it to the
astonished and delighted Sieglinde.)

Siegmund the Volsung
stands here, wife!
For bride-gift he
brings you this sword.
And thus he woos
the woman most blest.
He'll lead you from
the house of the foe.
Far from here
follow me now
out of the joyful
house of the spring:
your guard is Notung the Sword,
for Siegmund lies felled by your love.

(He puts his arm around her to take
her with him.)

SIEGLINDE

Are you Siegmund
standing beside me?
Sieglinde am I,
who longed for you,
your very sister
now won the same time as the sword!

SIEGMUND

Bride and sister
be to your brother—
Let Volsung blood bloom to the
world!

(He draws her to him in passionate
frenzy. She sinks to his breast with a
cry.)

ACT TWO

A Wild and Rocky Height

In the background a gorge slopes downward from a high peak, the ground
sinking again gradually from this
toward the foreground.

Wotan, in warlike array, is bearing his
spear; before him stands Brünnhilde,
fully armed as a Valkyr.

WOTAN

Now bridle your horse,
valorous maid!
Furious strife
soon will break out.
Brünnhilde, storm to the fight,
for now the Volsung must win!
Hunding has to choose
where he will go:
I ban him now from Valhall!
So up and away!
Ride to the field!

BRÜNNHILDE

(springing from rock to rock up the
height, and shouting)

Hoyotoho! Hoyotoho!
Heiaha! Heiaha!
Hahei! Hahei! Heiaho!

(She pauses on a high peak, looks down
into the ravine below and calls to
Wotan.)

I warn you, father,
ready yourself,
brave the storm
blowing this way.
Fricka's coming, your wife,
She's riding in her ram-driven car.
Hei! hear the golden
whip that she cracks!

SIEGLINDE (*ausser sich*)

War Wälse dein Vater,
und bist du ein Wälsung,
stiess er für dich
sein Schwert in den Stamm —
so lass mich dich heissen,
wie ich dich liebe:
Siegmund —
so nenn ich dich!

SIEGMUND

(*eilt auf den Stamm zu und fasst
den Schwertgriff*)

Siegmund heiss ich
und Siegmund bin ich!
Bezeug' es dies Schwert,
das zaglos ich halte!
Wälse verhiess mir,
in höchster Not
fänd' ich es einst:
ich fass' es nun!
Heiligster Minne
höchste Not,
sehnender Liebe
sehrende Not
brennt mir hell in der Brust,
drängt zu Tat und Tod:
Notung! Notung! —
so nenn ich dich, Schwert.
Notung! Notung!
neidlicher Stahl!
Zeig deiner Schärfe
schneidenden Zahn:
heraus aus der Scheide zu mir!

(*Er zieht mit einem gewaltigen Zuck
das Schwert aus dem Stamme und
zeigt es der von Staunen und Ent-
zücken erfassten Sieglinde.*)

Siegmund, den Wälsung,
siehst du, Weib!
Als Brautgabe
bringt er dies Schwert:
so freit er sich
die seligste Frau;
dem Feindeshaus
entführt er dich so.
Fern von hier
folge mir nun,
fort in des Lenzes
lachendes Haus:
dort schützt dich Notung, das Schwert,
wenn Siegmund dir liebend erlag!

(*Er hat sie umfasst, um sie mit sich
fortzuziehen.*)

SIEGLINDE

Bist du Siegmund,
den ich hier sehe —
Sieglinde bin ich,
die dich ersehnt:
die eigne Schwester
gewannst du zu eins mit dem Schwert!

SIEGMUND

Braut und Schwester
bist du dem Bruder —
so blühe denn Wälsungen-Blut!

(*Er zieht sie mit wütender Glut un sich,
sie sinkt mit einem Schrei an seine
Brust.*)

ZWEITER AUFZUG

Wildes Felsengebirge

*Im Hintergrunde zieht sich von unten
her eine Schlucht herauf, die auf ein
erhöhtes Felsjoch mündet; von die-
sem senkt sich der Boden dem Vordergrund zu wieder abwärts.*

*Wotan, kriegerisch gewaffnet, mit dem
Speer; vor ihm Brünnhilde, als
Walküre, ebenfalls in voller Waffen-
rüstung.*

WOTAN

Nun zäume dein Ross,
reisige Maid!
Bald entbrennt
brünstiger Streit:
Brünnhilde stürme zum Kampf,
dem Wälsung kiese sie Sieg!
Hunding wähle sich,
wem er gehört;
nach Walhall taugt er mir nicht.
Drum rüstig und rasch
reite zur Wal!

BRÜNNHILDE

(*jauchzend von Fels zu Fels die Höhe
rechts hinaufspringend*)

Hojotoho! Hojotoho!
Heiaha! Heiaha!
Hojotoho! Heiaha!

(*Sie hält auf einer hohen Felsspitze an,
blickt in die hintere Schlucht hinab
und ruft zu Wotan zurück.*)

Dir rat ich, Vater,
rüste dich selbst;
harten Sturm
sollst du besteh'n.
Fricka naht, deine Frau,
im Wagen mit dem Widdergespann.
Hei, wie die gold'ne
Geissel sie schwingt!

The wretched beasts are
groaning in fear.
I hear the wheels rattle.
How she rides for the brawl!
Such strife as this
is not to my taste!
Better the valorous
wars of men.
Take care, try to weather the storm.
I willingly leave you to fate!
Hoyotoho! Hoyotoho!
Heiaha! Heiaha!
Hoyotoho! Hoyotoho!
Heiaha! Heiaha!
Hoyotoho! Hoyotoho!
Hoyotoho! Hoyotoho!
Heiahaha!

(*She vanishes behind the rocks, as
Fricka enters from the heights after
ascending from the ravine in her
chariot drawn by two rams, alights
quickly and strides angrily toward
Wotan.*)

WOTAN

The same old storm!
The same old woe!
And yet here I must face it.

FRICKA

Though you hid among the hills
to miss the eyes of your wife,
still I came,
all by myself,
to get your promised assistance.

WOTAN

Reveal your troubles,
Fricka, my love.

FRICKA

I perceived Hunding's need.
He called me, craving revenge.
So wedding's guardian
lent her ear,
and gave pledge
to punish the deed
the bad, impudent pair
so boldly did to the spouse.

WOTAN

Was these mortals' deed so bad
whom spring united in love?
An ardent magic
entranced the two.
I ask no amends for love.

FRICKA

How stupid and dumb you would seem,
as though you were not aware
that when one flaunts the
holiest vows
of wedlock, I must lament it.

WOTAN

Unholy
always the vow
that joins those that lack love.
And now truly,
do not expect
me to put a stop
the thing you cannot;
for where keen fires are raging
I say quite frankly, just fight!

FRICKA

Since you look lightly
on wedlock's breach,
go prattle still further,
and call it holy
that incest should bloom forth
from bond of a twin-born pair.
My heart is aghast,
my mind's in a whirl.
Wedlock unites
the sister and brother.
When has it been heard
that sister and brother did marry?

WOTAN

So—hear of it now.
Endure then thus
what has been ordained,
though till now it has never been so.
They love one another—
that you know well—
so hear my honest advice!
If bliss is yours
as reward for your blessing,
then bless them, glad for the love that
makes these two beings as one.

FRICKA

It reached a sad pass
with the gods everlasting
when you begat the
violent Volsungs!
I speak plainly—
have I hit home?
You look on our lofty
race as a mockery.
You cast off all that
you once held in honor.
You've broken the bonds that
you made in the first place—
loosed while laughing

Die armen Tiere
ächzen vor Angst;
wild rasseln die Räder;
zornig fährt sie zum Zank!
In solchem Strausse
streit' ich nicht gern,
lieb' ich auch mutiger
Männer Schlacht.
Drum sieh, wie den Sturm du bestehst:
ich Lustige lass dich im Stich!
Hojotoho! Hojotoho!
Heiaha! Heiaha!
Heiahaha!

(*Brünnhilde verschwindet hinter der
Gebirgshöhe zur Seite. In einem mit
zwei Widdern bespannten Wagen
langt Fricka aus der Schlucht auf
dem Felsjoche an: dort hält sie rasch
an und steigt aus. Sie schreitet heftig
in den Vordergrund auf Wotan zu.*)

WOTAN

Der alte Sturm,
die alte Müh'!
Doch stand muss ich hier halten!

FRICKA

Wo in den Bergen du dich birgst,
der Gattin Blick zu entgehn,
einsam hier
such' ich dich auf,
dass Hilfe du mir verhiessest.

WOTAN

Was Fricka kümmert,
künde sie frei.

FRICKA

Ich vernahm Hundings Not,
um Rache rief er mich an:
der Ehe Hüterin
hörte ihn,
verhiess streng
zu strafen die Tat
des frech frevelnden Paar's,
das kühn den Gatten gekränkt.

WOTAN

Was so Schlimmes
schuf das Paar,
das liebend einte der Lenz?
Der Minne Zauber
entzückte sie:
wer büsst mir der Minne Macht?

FRICKA

Wie töricht und taub du dich stellst,
als wüsstest fürwahr du nicht,
dass um der Ehe
heiligen Eid,
den hart gekränkten, ich klage!

WOTAN

Unheilig
acht ich den Eid,
der Unliebende eint;
und mir wahrlich
mute nicht zu,
dass mit Zwang ich halte,
was dir nicht haftet:
denn wo kühn Kräfte sich regen,
da rat' ich offen zum Krieg.

FRICKA

Achtest du rühmlich
der Ehe Bruch,
so prahle nun weiter
und preis' es heilig,
dass Blutschande entblüht
dem Bund eines Zwillingspaars!
Mir schaudert das Herz,
es schwindelt mein Hirn:
bräutlich umfing
die Schwester der Bruder!
Wann ward es erlebt,
dass leiblich Geschwister sich liebten?

WOTAN

Heut' — hast du's erlebt!
Erfahre so,
was von selbst sich fügt,
sei zuvor auch noch nie es gescheh'n.
Dass jene sich lieben,
leuchtet dir hell;
drum höre redlichen Rat:
Soll süsse Lust
deinen Segen dir lohnen,
so segne, lachend, der Liebe,
Siegmunds und Sieglinds Bund!

FRICKA

So ist es denn aus
mit den ewigen Göttern,
seit du die wilden
Wälsungen zeugtest?
Heraus sagt' ich's;
traf ich den Sinn?
Nichts gilt dir der Hehren
heilige Sippe;
hin wirfst du alles,
was einst du geachtet;
zerreissest die Bande,
die selbst du gebunden,
lösest lachend

the hold of heaven,
so your silly, rascally couple,
the sensual fruit of sin,
can just revel and wanton at will.
Yet why worry for
wedlock and vows
which yourself were first to defame!
You've always wronged
your virtuous wife.
Never a depth and
never a height but
therein peeped and
lusted your look.
With your urge for change ever growing,
your scorn has harrowed my heart.
Sad were the thoughts
pent up in my bosom
when off you marched
with those wretched maidens
your lawless love had
brought to the world.
Yet you've showed such fear of your
  wife
that the Valkyrie band,
and Brünnhild herself—
who is near your heart—
you have ordered to listen to me.
But now that new names have
taken your fancy,
you roam the forest
as Volsa the wolfish!
Then when you've sunk to the
depths of your shame,
you beget a couple
of commonplace mortals.
Now the wife of your vows
is flung at the feet of your whelps!
So finish your work!
Fill up my cup:
The betrayed one now must be
  trampled!

WOTAN (*calmly*)

You've never learned—
though I would teach you—
the things you can't comprehend,
for first they have to take place.
All you know is
the commonplace things,
whereas my thoughts foresee
the events yet to come.
One thing, mark you:
need brings a man
who, free from godly protection,
is free from the laws of the gods.
Only such can
accomplish the deed,
which, though gods would perform it,
no god dare perform for himself.

FRICKA

Your thoughts are deep and
meant to confuse me.
What lofty deed can
hero accomplish
that by the gods is not to be done,
by whose grace alone he can work?

WOTAN

Does his own plain courage
count not at all?

FRICKA

Who breathed the life into men,
gave light to who hardly could see.
They seem quite strong,
aided by you.
and when you goad them,
truly they strive.
You—you alone goad them.
The god then says they are good!
With new deceits
you would still evade me,
with new devices
still would outrun me.
And yet this Volsung
shall never be yours.
I can strike you through him.
He is bold only through you.

WOTAN

His woes were wild,
and he grew by himself.
My arm shielded him not.

FRICKA

Then shield him not today.
Take back the sword
you gave to him once.

WOTAN

The sword?

FRICKA

Yes, the sword,
that ready sword,
magic in might,
that you, god, did grant your son.

WOTAN

Siegmund achieved it himself
in his need.

FRICKA

You shaped both his need
and the sword of his need.
Would you deceive me,
who day and night
followed close on your heels?
For him you did thrust
the sword in the tree,

des Himmels Haft:
dass nach Lust und Laune nur walte
dies frevelnde Zwillingspaar,
deiner Untreue zuchtlose Frucht!
O, was klag' ich
um Ehe und Eid,
da zuerst du selbst sie versehrt.
Die treue Gattin
trogest du stets;
wo eine Tiefe,
wo eine Höhe,
dahin lugte
lüstern dein Blick,
wie des Wechsels Lust du gewännest
und höhnend kränktest mein Herz.
Trauernden Sinnes
musst' ich's ertragen,
zogst du zur Schlacht
mit den schlimmen Mädchen,
die wilder Minne
Bund dir gebar:
denn dein Weib noch scheutest du so,
dass der Walküren Schar
und Brünnhilde selbst,
deines Wunsches Braut,
in Gehorsam der Herrin du gabst.
Doch jetzt, da dir neue
Namen gefielen,
als "Wälse" wölfisch
im Walde du schweiftest;
jetzt, da zu niedrigster
Schmach du dich neigtest,
gemeiner Menschen
ein Paar zu erzeugen:
jetzt dem Wurfe der Wölfin
wirfst du zu Füssen dein Weib!
So führ es denn aus!
Fülle das Mass!
Die Betrogne lass auch zertreten!

WOTAN (*ruhig*)

Nichts lerntest du,
wollt' ich dich lehren,
was nie du erkennen kannst,
eh' nicht ertagte die Tat.
Stets Gewohntes
nur magst du versteh'n:
doch was noch nie sich traf,
danach trachtet mein Sinn.
Eines höre!
Not tut ein Held,
der, ledig göttlichen Schutzes,
sich löse vom Göttergesetz.
So nur taugt er,
zu wirken die Tat,
die, wie not sie den Göttern,
dem Gott doch zu wirken verwehrt.

FRICKA

Mit tiefem Sinne
willst du mich täuschen:
was Hehres sollten
Helden je wirken,
das ihren Göttern wäre verwehrt,
deren Gunst in ihnen nur wirkt?

WOTAN

Ihres eignen Mutes
achtest du nicht?

FRICKA

Wer hauchte Menschen ihn ein?
Wer hellte den Blöden den Blick?
In deinem Schutz
scheinen sie stark,
durch deinen Stachel
streben sie auf:
du reizest sie einzig,
die so mir Ew'gen du rühmst.
Mit neuer List
willst du mich belügen,
durch neue Ränke
mir jetzt entrinnen;
doch diesen Wälsung
gewinnst du dir nicht:
in ihm treff' ich nur dich,
denn durch dich trotzt er allein.

WOTAN

In wildem Leiden
erwuchs er sich selbst:
mein Schutz schirmte ihn nie.

FRICKA

So schütz' auch heut' ihn nicht!
Nimm ihm das Schwert,
das du ihm geschenkt!

WOTAN

Das Schwert?

FRICKA

Ja, das Schwert,
das zauberstark
zuckende Schwert,
das du Gott dem Sohne gabst.

WOTAN

Siegmund gewann es sich
selbst in der Not.

FRICKA

Du schufst ihm die Not
wie das neidliche Schwert.
Willst du mich täuschen,
die Tag und Nacht
auf den Fersen dir folgt?
Für ihn stiessest du
das Schwert in den Stamm,

and you promised him
the noble steel.
Can you deny it
was only your art
that brought him where it was found?
A noble will
fight not a vassal.
Such rogues are only for whipping.
Fight against your force:
that I might do;
but Siegmund is only a knave.
Shall he who owes you
service and homage
be master now
of the goddess, your wife?
Shall one so base
outrageously shame me,
a varlet dictatè,
a ruler obey?
My husband cannot desire it.
He would not dishonor his queen.

WOTAN

What then would you?

FRICKA

Give up the Volsung.

WOTAN (*with choked voice*)

He goes his own way.

FRICKA

Why then—give him no aid,
when the foe calls for vengeance due.

WOTAN

I'll—give him no aid.

FRICKA

Look at me plainly.
Plan no deceit.
Just keep Brünnhild out of his way.

WOTAN

The Valkyrie rules herself.

FRICKA

Not yet. It is your will
alone she obeys.
Forbid her to help him win.

WOTAN

I cannot destroy him:
he found my sword.

FRICKA

Get rid of the magic,
his weapon will break.
Let him fight without arms!

BRÜNNHILDE'S VOICE

Heiaha! Heiaha!
Hoyotoho!
(*The Valkyrie appears with her steed
on the rocky path.*)

FRICKA

Here comes your audacious maid.
Hear the joy in her voice!

BRÜNNHILDE

Heiaha! Heiaha!
Hoyohotoyo! Hotoyoha!

WOTAN (*aside*)

I called her for Siegmund to horse.

FRICKA

Let her shield today
Protect the fair honor
of Wotan's holy wife.
A mock to mankind.
and shorn of our might
even we gods will be doomed,
if this day your valiant
maid fails to champion
my high and legitimate rights.
Your son must die for my honor.
Will Wotan so pledge me his oath?

WOTAN

(*throwing himself upon a rocky seat in
utter dejection and inward rage*)

Take the oath!

FRICKA (*to Brünnhilde*)

Lord father waits for you.
Let him inform you
how the lot has been cast.
(*She mounts her car and drives off.*)

BRÜNNHILDE

(*advances with anxious and wondering
look toward Wotan, who, head on
hand, is absorbed in gloomy re-
flection*)

Ill, likely,
soon will come:
Fricka laughed at the outcome.
Father, what must your child
experience?
Crushed you seem, and unhappy.

WOTAN

The chains I welded
now hold me fast—
least free of all beings.

BRÜNNHILDE

You never were thus.
What gnaws at your heart?

du verhiessest ihm
die hehre Wehr:
willst du es leugnen,
dass nur deine List
ihn lockte, wo er es fänd'?
Mit Unfreien
streitet kein Edler,
den Frevler straft nur der Freie.
Wider deine Kraft
führt' ich wohl Krieg:
doch Siegmund verfiel mir als Knecht!
Der dir als Herren
hörig und eigen,
gehorchen soll ihm
dein ewig Gemahl?
Soll mich in Schmach
der Niedrigste schmähen,
dem Frechen zum Sporn,
dem Freien zum Spott?
Das kann mein Gatte nicht wollen,
die Göttin entweiht er nicht so!

WOTAN
Was verlangst du?

FRICKA
Lass von dem Wälsung!

WOTAN
(mit gedämpfter Stimme)
Er geh' seines Weg's.

FRICKA
Doch du schütze ihn nicht,
wenn zur Schlacht ihn der Rächer ruft!

WOTAN
Ich schütze ihn nicht.

FRICKA
Sieh mir ins Auge,
sinne nicht Trug:
die Walküre wend' auch von ihm!

WOTAN
Die Walküre walte frei.

FRICKA
Nicht doch; deinen Willen
vollbringt sie allein:
verbiete ihr Siegmunds Sieg!

WOTAN
Ich kann ihn nicht fällen:
er fand mein Schwert!

FRICKA
Entzieh' dem den Zauber,
zerknick es dem Knecht!
Schutzlos schau ihn der Feind!

BRÜNNHILDE
(noch unsichtbar von der Höhe her)
Heiaha! Heiaha! Hojotoho!
(Brünnhilde erscheint mit ihrem Ross
auf dem Felsenpfade rechts.)

FRICKA
Dort kommt deine kühne Maid;
jauchzend jagt sie daher.

BRÜNNHILDE
Heiaha! Heiaha!
Heiohotojo! Hotojoha!

WOTAN (für sich)
Ich rief sie für Siegmund zu Ross!

FRICKA
Deiner ew'gen Gattin
heilige Ehre
beschirme heut ihr Schild!
Von Menschen verlacht,
verlustig der Macht,
gingen wir Götter zugrund:
würde heut' nicht hehr
und herrlich mein Recht
gerächt von der mutigen Maid.
Der Wälsung fällt meiner Ehre!
Empfah' ich von Wotan den Eid?

WOTAN
(in furchtbarem Unmut und innerem
Grimm auf einen Felsensitz sich
werfend)
Nimm den Eid!

FRICKA (zu Brünnhilde)
Heervater harret dein:
lass ihn dir künden,
wie das Los er gekiest!
(Sie besteigt den Wagen und fährt
schnell davon.)

BRÜNNHILDE
(tritt mit besorgter Miene vor Wotan,
der, auf dem Felssitz zurückgelehnt,
das Haupt auf die Hand gestützt, in
finsteres Brüten versunken ist.)
Schlimm, fürcht ich,
schloss der Streit,
lachte Fricka dem Lose.
Vater, was soll
dein Kind erfahren?
Trübe scheinst du und traurig!

WOTAN
In eigner Fessel
fing ich mich,
ich Unfreiester aller!

BRÜNNHILDE
So sah ich dich nie!
Was nagt dir das Herz?

WOTAN

O, greatest of shame!
O, shamefulest woe!
Gods have grief!
Gods have grief!
Infinite wrath!
Endless despair!
The saddest I am of all beings!

BRÜNNHILDE

(in alarm, throws away her shield,
spear and helmet, and sinks at
Wotan's feet)
Father! Father!
Tell me, what is it?
You are filling your child with alarm!
Have trust in me,
your daughter true.
See, Brünnhild is pleading.

(She lays her head and hands confid-
ingly and anxiously on his knees and
breast.)

WOTAN

(He gazes long into her face and strokes
her hair. Then, as if coming to himself again, he at last begins in a very
low voice.)
Yet if I tell it,
might I not lose
the controlling power of my will?

BRÜNNHILDE

To Wotan's will you're speaking,
telling me what you will.
What am I,
if I am not your will?

WOTAN

What never was uttered to any
will stay unuttered,
now and forever.
Myself I speak to,
speaking to you.
When young love vanished
with its delights,
my spirit aspired to power,
and spurred by former
wishes, I went
and won myself the world.
I thought no falsehood,
yet I did falsely,
carried out contracts
where harm lay hid.
Wandering Loge did lure me,
then left me in the lurch.
But the urge for love
still had some power.
In my might I longed for affection.
In night was born
the fearsome Nibelung.

Alberich broke through its law,
by cursing at love;
so he won through the curse
the glittering gold of the Rhine,
and with it measureless might.
I ravished the ring
he cunningly fashioned
yet it did not
go back to the Rhine:
with it I paid for
Valhall's ramparts,
the fort the giants have built me,
from which I hold rule of the world.
The one who knows
all things that were,
Erda, the wisest
holiest Vala,
warned me off from the ring,
told me of doom that was coming.
I desired to know more
of this future;
but silent, she vanished away.
Then I lost all my peace of mind.
The god was still eager to know.
To the womb of the earth
downward did I go:
with love's strong magic
conquered the Vala,
toppled her wisdom's pride,
so she told me what would come.
Tidings I heard from her lips:
I gave her a token while there:
most wise woman on earth,
she bore me, Brünnhilde—you.
And eight sisters
grew up with you
with such Valkyrs, I
hoped to break
the fate which the Vala
had bade me dread—
the gods' ignominious downfall.
I wanted might
to conquer the foe,
so you were sent to find heroes:
the men we once ruled
by our laws, so proudly,
the men, whose courage
we curbed and suppressed,
whom through cloudy, deceitful,
villainous compacts
we bound to a blind and
a servile obedience—
your work is to spur
and prick on their valor,
and by that rouse them
to savage war,
so valiant warrior troops may
be marshaled in Valhall's hall.

WOTAN

O heilige Schmach!
O schmählicher Harm!
Götternot!
Götternot!
Endloser Grimm!
Ewiger Gram!
Der Traurigste bin ich von allen!

BRÜNNHILDE

(*wirft erschrocken Schild, Speer und
Helm von sich und lässt sich mit
besorgter Zutraulichkeit zu Wotans
Füssen nieder*)

Vater! Vater!
Sage, was ist dir?
Wie erschreckst du mit Sorge dein
    Kind?
Vertraue mir!
Ich bin dir treu:
sieh, Brünnhilde bittet!

(*Sie legt traulich und ängstlich Haupt
und Hände ihm auf Knie und
Schoss.*)

WOTAN

(*blickt ihr lange ins Auge; dann
streichelt er ihr die Locken. Wie aus
tiefem Sinnen zu sich kommend, be-
ginnt er leise*)

Lass' ich's verlauten,
lös' ich dann nicht
meines Willens haltenden Haft?

BRÜNNHILDE

Zu Wotans Willen sprichst du,
sagst du mir, was du willst;
wer bin ich,
wär' ich dein Wille nicht?

WOTAN

Was keinem in Worten ich künde,
unausgesprochen
bleib' es denn ewig:
mit mir nur rat' ich,
red' ich zu dir.
Als junger Liebe
Lust mir verblich,
verlangte nach Macht mein Mut:
von jäher Wünsche
Wüten gejagt,
gewann ich mir die Welt.
Unwissend trugvoll,
Untreue übt' ich,
band durch Verträge,
was Unheil barg:
listig verlockte mich Loge,
der schweifend nun verschwand.
Von der Liebe doch
mocht' ich nicht lassen,
in der Macht verlangt' ich nach Minne.
Den Nacht gebar,
der bange Nibelung,

Alberich, brach ihren Bund;
er fluchte der Lieb'
und gewann durch den Fluch
des Rheines glänzendes Gold
und mit ihm masslose Macht.
Den Ring, den er schuf,
entriss ich ihm listig;
doch nicht dem Rhein
gab ich ihn zurück:
mit ihm bezahlt' ich
Walhalls Zinnen,
der Burg, die Riesen mir bauten,
aus der ich der Welt nun gebot.
Die alles weiss,
was einstens war,
Erda, die weihlich
weiseste Wala,
riet mir ab von dem Ring,
warnte vor ewigem Ende.
Von dem Ende wollt' ich
mehr noch wissen;
doch schweigend entschwand mir **das**
    Weib.
Da verlor ich den leichten Mut,
zu wissen begehrt' es den Gott:
in den Schoss der Welt
schwang ich mich hinab
mit Liebeszauber
zwang ich die Wala,
stört' ihres Wissens Stolz,
dass sie Rede nun mir stand.
Kunde empfing ich von ihr;
von mir doch barg sie ein Pfand:
der Welt weisestes Weib
gebar mir, Brünnhilde, dich.
Mit acht Schwestern
zog ich dich auf;
durch euch Walküren
wollt' ich wenden,
was mir die Wala
zu fürchten schuf:
ein schmähliches Ende der Ew'gen.
Dass stark zum Streit
uns fände der Feind,
hiess ich euch Helden mir schaffen:
die herrisch wir sonst
in Gesetzen hielten,
die Männer, denen
den Mut wir gewehrt,
die durch trüber Verträge
trügende Bande
zu blindem Gehorsam
wir uns gebunden —
die solltet zu Sturm
und Streit ihr nun stacheln,
ihre Kraft reizen
zu rauhem Krieg,
dass kühner Kämpfer Scharen
ich sammle in Walhalls Saal!

BRÜNNHILDE

We have filled Valhall with heroes;
many I brought you myself.
So why are you troubled?
We never let up.

WOTAN

It's something else—
mark my words well—
something the Vala foretold!
For Alberich's host
threatens our downfall:
the envious dwarf
mutters with rancor;
and yet I've no fear
of his armies of darkness,
for my heroes make me secure.
But if once the ring
were won by the Nibelung—
then would our Valhall be ended.
He who curses love, he,
he alone
knows the magic
the ring possesses,
and so can will
the doom of the gods.
He seeks to turn
my heroes from me,
and when he wins
my men to his will,
to urge them on
to battle with me.
Anguish taught me the way
to wrest the ring from his clutches.
I gave a giant
payment one time
with accursed gold
for work he did.
Fafner guards now the hoard
he won from the brother he slew.
I must get the circlet from him,
which I myself used to pay him.
But I honor my word,
so dare not attack him.
Mightless by law,
my spirit is gone.
These are the fetters
that now bind me.
I who by treaties was lord,
by these treaties now am a slave.
Yet one can manage
what I don't dare,
a hero, never
helped by my power;
who, strange to gods, is
free of their grace;
on his own,
not at their beck,
his need his own,

and his arms his own—
this one can do
what I fear to try,
and never urged him do
though it was all of my wish.
One who'd battle the god,
yet would serve me,
a favorable foe—
ah, where is he found?
How bring forth a freeman
I've never aided,
who despite defiance
is dear to my heart?
Now could I create one
who not through me,
but through himself would
express my will?
O, need of the gods!
terrible shame!
I feel disgust just
seeing myself
in all the deeds I accomplish!
The other, that I have longed for,
the other I never see.
The free are their only creators—
Varlets are all I can make!

BRÜNNHILDE

Yet the Volsung, Siegmund,
is he not free?

WOTAN

Both together
we roamed the forest.
Boldly, I brought him up to
flaunt the laws of the gods—
only the sword can save him
now from the wrath of the gods,
and that, in favor,
came from a god!
Why did I want to
trick myself this way?
How easily Fricka
found out the fraud!
She saw right through me,
all to my shame!
I must yield my will to her purpose.

BRÜNNHILDE

So Siegmund must fall in the fight?

WOTAN

I have handled Alberich's ring—
grasped the gold in my greed!
The curse that I fled
will flee not from me.
What I love I now must surrender,
murder what most I've cherished,
basely betray the
one who trusts!

BRÜNNHILDE
Deinen Saal füllten wir weidlich:
viele schon führt' ich dir zu.
Was macht dir nun Sorge,
da nie wir gesäumt?

WOTAN
Ein andres ist's:
achte es wohl,
wes' mich die Wala gewarnt!
Durch Alberichs Heer
droht uns das Ende:
mit neidischem Grimm
grollt mir der Nib'lung:
doch scheu ich nun nicht
seine nächtigen Scharen,
meine Helden schüfen mir Sieg.
Nur wenn je den Ring
zurück er gewänne,
dann wäre Walhall verloren:
der der Liebe fluchte,
er allein
nützte neidisch
des Ringes Runen
zu aller Edlen
endloser Schmach;
der Helden Mut
entwendet' er mir;
die Kühnen selber
zwäng er zum Kampf;
mit ihrer Kraft
bekriegte er mich.
Sorgend sann ich nun selbst,
den Ring dem Feind zu entreissen.
Der Riesen einer,
denen ich einst
mit verfluchtem Gold
den Fleiss vergalt:
Fafner hütet den Hort,
um den er den Bruder gefällt.
Ihm müsst' den Reif ich entringen,
den selbst als Zoll ich ihm zahlte.
Doch mit dem ich vertrug,
ihn darf ich nicht treffen;
machtlos vor ihm
erläge mein Mut:
das sind die Bande,
die mich binden:
der durch Verträge ich Herr,
den Verträgen bin ich nun Knecht.
Nur einer könnte,
was ich nicht darf:
ein Held, dem helfend
nie ich mich neigte;
der fremd dem Gotte,
frei seiner Gunst,
unbewusst,
ohne Geheiss,
aus eigner Not,

mit der eignen Wehr
schüfe die Tat,
die scheuen ich muss,
die nie mein Rat ihm riet,
wünscht sie auch einzig mein Wunsch!
Der, entgegen dem Gott,
für mich föchte,
den freundlichen Feind,
wie fände ich ihn?
Wie schüf' ich den Freien,
den nie ich schirmte,
der in eignem Trotze
der Trauteste mir?
Wie macht' ich den andren,
der nicht mehr ich,
und aus sich wirkte,
was ich nur will?
O göttliche Not!
Grässliche Schmach!
Zum Ekel find ich
ewig nur mich
in allem, was ich erwirke!
Das andre, das ich ersehne,
das andre erseh' ich nie:
denn selbst muss der Freie sich
    schaffen;
Knechte erknet ich mir nur!

BRÜNNHILDE
Doch der Wälsung, Siegmund,
wirkt er nicht selbst?

WOTAN
Wild durchschweift' ich
mit ihm die Wälder;
gegen der Götter Rat
reizte kühn ich ihn auf:
gegen der Götter Rache
schützt ihn nun einzig das Schwert,
das eines Gottes
Gunst ihm beschied.
Wie wollt' ich listig
selbst mich belügen?
So leicht ja entfrug mir
Fricka den Trug:
zu tiefster Scham
durchschaute sie mich!
Ihrem Willen muss ich gewähren.

BRÜNNHILDE
So nimmst du von Siegmund den Sieg?

WOTAN
Ich berührte Alberichs Ring,
gierig hielt ich das Gold!
Der Fluch, den ich floh,
nicht flieht er nun mich:
Was ich liebe, muss ich verlassen,
morden, wen je ich minne,
trügend verraten
wer mir traut!

Farewell to you,
glorious pomp,
godly pretense's,
glittering shame!
So let it perish—
all I have built!
So I end my work,
and wait for just one thing:
the finish—
the finish!
(*He pauses in meditation.*)
And for that finish
looks Alberich!
Now I've fathomed
the secret sense
of Vala's maddening riddle:
"When the darksome foe of love
wrathful, brings forth a son,
the blest one's end
will linger not!"
A rumor told
a tale of the dwarf,
that he'd won himself a woman,
his gold gaining her grace.
The fruit of hate
soon is to come.
The seed of spite
grows in her womb.
This wonder befell
the loveless Nibelung!
But I have never brought forth
a free one, although I have loved.
(*grimly*)
So take of my blessing,
Nibelungen son!
What deeply grieves me
is yours to inherit;
my godhood's empty display;
so gnaw away, glutting your greed.

BRÜNNHILDE (*in terror*)

Oh, say, tell me,
what must your child do?

WOTAN (*bitterly*)

Fight strictly for Fricka,
guard holy wedlock's laws!
The choice she made,
is also my own.
The will that I work is worthless,
for my will can't bring forth a free man.
Help Fricka's vassals
when there is strife!

BRÜNNHILDE

Woe! Have pity!
Retract your words!
You love Siegmund.
For your sake—
I know it—I shall protect him.

WOTAN

Put an end to Siegmund,
for Hunding must win in the strife.
Watch yourself well,
maintain your control.
Put forth your prowess
to further his fight.
A charmed sword
helps Siegmund.
Strength and valor is his!

BRÜNNHILDE

One you have taught me
always to love
who in lofty virtue
is dear to your bosom
never will find me hostile
through your two-faced word!

WOTAN

Ha, shameless one!
This is your taunt?
Who are you, if not the blind and
tame tool of my will?
When I told my sorrows
did I so sink
as to be a mock to
the being I made?
Does my child know my wrath?
Your spirit would quail
if I were ever
to hurl bolts of my fire!
Within my bosom
smoulders a hate
which could send forth
horrors on the world
that once was all my delight.
Woe to him whom it hits!
Grief would pay for his pride!
So heed my words.
Rouse me not up.
Be sure you hark to my hest:
death to Siegmund!
This be the Valkyrie's work.

(*He storms away, vanishing in the
    mountains.*)

BRÜNNHILDE

Father was never like this,
although he oft was quick in wrath.

(*She stands a while stunned.*)

How heavy
my weapons' weight!
When I loved the fight,
how light they did seem!
This evil strife
makes me fear my task!

(*She ponders and sighs.*)

Fahre denn hin,
herrische Pracht,
göttlichen Prunkes
prahlende Schmach!
Zusammenbreche,
was ich gebaut!
Auf geb', ich mein Werk;
nur eines will ich noch:
das Ende,
das Ende!
(*Er hält sinnend ein.*)
Und für das Ende
sorgt Alberich!
Jetzt versteh' ich
den stummen Sinn
des wilden Wortes der Wala:
"Wenn der Liebe finstrer Feind
zürnend zeugt einen Sohn,
der Sel'gen Ende
säumt dann nicht!"
Vom Nib'lung jüngst
vernahm ich die Mär,
dass ein Weib der Zwerg bewältigt,
des Gunst Gold ihm erzwang:
des Hasses Frucht
hegt eine Frau,
des Neides Kraft
kreisst ihm im Schoss:
das Wunder gelang
dem Liebelosen;
doch der in Lieb' ich freite,
den Freien erlang' ich mir nicht.
(*mit bitterem Grimm sich
aufrichtend*)
So nimm meinen Segen,
Nib'lungen-Sohn!
Was tief mich ekelt,
dir geb ich's zum Erbe,
der Gottheit nichtigen Glanz:
zernage ihn gierig dein Neid!

BRÜNNHILDE (*erschrocken*)
O sag', künde,
was soll nun dein Kind?

WOTAN (*bitter*)
Fromm streite für Fricka;
hüte ihr Eh' und Eid!
Was sie erkor,
das kiese auch ich:
was frommte mir eigner Wille?
Einen Freien kann ich nicht wollen:
für Frickas Knechte
kämpfe nun du!

BRÜNNHILDE
Weh! Nimm reuig
zurück das Wort!
Du liebst Siegmund;
dir zulieb,
ich weiss es, schütz' ich den Wälsung.

WOTAN
Fällen sollst du Siegmund,
für Hunding erfechten den Sieg!
Hüte dich wohl
und halte dich stark,
all deiner Kühnheit
entbiete im Kampf:
ein Siegschwert
schwingt Siegmund;
schwerlich fällt er dir feig'!

BRÜNNHILDE
Den du zu lieben
stets mich gelehrt,
der in hehrer Tugend
dem Herzen dir teuer —
gegen ihn zwingt mich nimmer
dein zwiespältig' Wort!

WOTAN
Ha, Freche du!
Frevelst du mir?
Wer bist du, als meines Willens
blind wählende Kür?
Da mit dir ich tagte,
sank ich so tief,
dass zum Schimpf der eignen
Geschöpfe ich ward?
Kennst du, Kind, meinen Zorn?
Verzage dein Mut,
wenn je zermalmend
auf dich stürzte sein Strahl!
In meinem Busen
berg' ich den Grimm,
der in Grau'n und Wust
wirft eine Welt,
die einst zur Lust mir gelacht:
Wehe dem, den er trifft!
Trauer schüf' ihm sein Trotz!
Drum rat ich dir,
reize mich nicht!
Besorge, was ich befahl:
Siegmund falle!
Dies sei der Walküre Werk!
(*Er stürmt fort und verschwindet im
Gebirge.*)

BRÜNNHILDE
So sah ich Siegvater nie,
(*Sie starrt wild vor sich hin.*)
erzürnt' ihn sonst wohl auch ein Zank!
Schwer wiegt mir
der Waffen Wucht.
Wenn nach Lust ich focht,
wie waren sie leicht!
Zu böser Schlacht
schleich ich heut so bang.
(*Sie sinnt vor sich hin und seufzt dann
auf.*)
Weh, mein Wälsung!

Woe, my Volsung!
In greatest need
I must falsely abandon the true one!

(*She looks up to see Siegmund and
Sieglinde ascending from the gorge.
She watches them a moment and
then re-enters the cave to her horse.
Siegmund and Sieglinde enter. She
presses hastily forward; he seeks to
restrain her.*)

SIEGMUND

Rest here a while;
take some repose!

SIEGLINDE

Onward! Onward!

SIEGMUND (*putting his arm around her,
firmly but tenderly*)

No farther now!
Just wait, O sweetest of wives!
You start from the rapture
love would arouse,
with sudden haste
hurrying forth,
so fast I can scarce pursue;
through wood and plain,
over rock and stone,
speechless, silent,
bounding along.
No call kept you from flight.
Rest for a while,
say just a word,
ending your silent woe!
See, your brother
holds you, his bride—
Siegmund now is your mate!

(*He has led her quietly to the rocky
seat.*)

SIEGLINDE

(*She gazes into Siegmund's eyes with
growing rapture, then mournfully
hangs upon his neck. Then she starts
up in sudden panic.*)

Away! Away!
Flee the profaned one!
Unholy
the clasp of her arm.
Disgraced, dishonored,
let me stay dead!
Flee this body,
let it alone!
May winds blow her away,
the foul one who followed the fair!
For he has given her love,
and blessedest joy was hers.
She loved her lover in full,

who gave in full of his love.
In the sweetest delights of
holiest raptures,
a piercing pain
struck senses and soul;
groanings and shudders
of shame and of terror
fastened their grip
and filled her with horror
to think she once had obeyed
a man she loved not at all!
Leave the accursed,
leave her to flee!
An outcast am I,
bereft of grace!
I now must leave him
the purest of manhood,
I dare not be yours
in love and obedience:
Shame would fall on my brother,
scorn on rescuing friend!

SIEGMUND

For all shame you have felt
the blood of the vile shall pay!
So flee now no farther.
Wait for the foeman.
Here—here I shall slay him:
when Notung's point
shall taste his heart.
Vengeance shall surely be yours!

SIEGLINDE
(*starting up and listening*)

Hark! The horn-calls—
Listen—those sounds!
All around,
raging and shrill
from wood and vale
clamors arise.
Hunding has wakened
from heavy sleep.
Kinsmen and bloodhounds have
come as he calls them.
Hear how the pack
howls in frenzy,
loud-baying to heaven
at the breaking of wedlock's fair vows!

(*She laughs wildly, then suddenly
shrinks in terror.*)

Where are you, Siegmund?
Are you still here?
Ardently loved and
radiant brother!
Let your starlit eyes
shine once more on me sweetly.
Spurn not the kiss
of the outcast, loving wife!
Hark! Oh, hark!

Im höchsten Leid
muss dich treulos die Treue verlassen!
(*Auf dem Bergjoch angelangt, gewahrt
Brünnhilde, in die Schlucht hinab-
blickend, Siegmund und Sieglinde;
sie betrachtet die Nahenden einen
Augenblick und wendet sich dann in
die Höhle zu ihrem Ross. Siegmund
und Sieglinde erscheinen auf dem
Bergjoch. Sieglinde schreitet hastig
voraus; Siegmund sucht sie aufzu-
halten.*)

SIEGMUND

Raste nur hier;
gönne dir Ruh!

SIEGLINDE

Weiter! Weiter!

SIEGMUND

(*umfasst sie mit sanfter Gewalt*)
Nicht weiter nun!
Verweile, süssestes Weib!
Aus Wonne-Entzücken
zucktest du auf,
mit jäher Hast
jagtest du fort:
kaum folgt' ich der wilden Flucht;
durch Wald und Flur,
über Fels und Stein,
sprachlos, schweigend
sprangst du dahin,
kein Ruf hielt dich zur Rast!
Ruhe nun aus:
rede zu mir!
Ende des Schweigens Angst!
Sieh, dein Bruder
hält seine Braut:
Siegmund ist dir Gesell!
(*Er hat sie unvermerkt nach dem Stein-
sitze geleitet.*)

SIEGLINDE

(*blickt Siegmund mit wachsendem Ent-
zücken in die Augen; dann um-
schlingt sie leidenschaftlich seinen
Hals und verweilt so; dann fährt sie
mit jähem Schreck auf*)
Hinweg! Hinweg!
Flieh die Entweihte!
Unheilig
umfängt dich ihr Arm;
entehrt, geschändet
schwand dieser Leib:
flieh die Leiche,
lasse sie los!
Der Wind mag sie verwehn,
die ehrlos dem Edlen sich gab!
Da er sie liebend umfing,
da seligste Lust sie fand,
da ganz sie minnte der Mann,

der ganz ihre Minne geweckt:
vor der süssesten Wonne
heiligster Weihe,
die ganz ihr Sinn
und Seele durchdrang,
Grauen und Schauder
ob grässlichster Schande
musste mit Schreck
die Schmähliche fassen,
die je dem Manne gehorcht,
der ohne Minne sie hielt!
Lass die Verfluchte,
lass sie dich flieh'n!
Verworfen bin ich,
der Würde bar!
Dir reinstem Manne
muss ich entrinnen,
Dir Herrlichem darf ich
nimmer gehören.
Schande bring ich dem Bruder,
Schmach dem freienden Freund!

SIEGMUND

Was Schande je dir schuf,
das büsst nun des Frevlers Blut!
Drum fliehe nicht weiter;
harre des Feindes;
hier soll er mir fallen:
wenn Notung ihm
das Herz zernagt,
Rache dann hast du erreicht!

SIEGLINDE

(*schrickt auf und lauscht*)
Horch! die Hörner,
hörst du den Ruf?
Ringsher tönt
wütend' Getös';
aus Wald und Gau
gellt es herauf.
Hunding erwachte
aus hartem Schlaf!
Sippen und Hunde
ruft er zusammen;
mutig gehetzt
heult die Meute,
wild bellt sie zum Himmel
um der Ehe gebrochenen Eid!
(*Sieglinde starrt wie wahnsinnig vor
sich hin.*)
Wo bist du, Siegmund?
Seh' ich dich noch,
brünstig geliebter,
leuchtender Bruder?
Deines Auges Stern
lass noch einmal mir strahlen:
wehre dem Kuss
des verworf'nen Weibes nicht!
Horch, o horch!

That is Hunding's horn!
Hear his hounds come near
in mighty force!
No sword serves
when the pack attacks.
Drop your blade, Siegmund!
Siegmund—where are you?
Ah, there—I see you there—
Terrible sight!
Bloodhounds gnashing
their ravening fangs!
They pay no heed
to your noble glance.
And they maul your feet with
their terrible teeth—
You fall—
In pieces now lies your sword!
The ashtree splits—
its trunk is riven.
Brother! My brother!
Siegmund, ha!
(*She shrieks and falls senseless into Siegmund's arms.*)

SIEGMUND

Sister! Beloved!
(*He listens for her breathing until he knows that she still lives. He lowers her gently, seats himself and rests her head on his knee. After a pause he bends tenderly over her and impresses a long kiss on her brow.*)

BRÜNNHILDE

(*Leading her steed by the bridle, she enters slowly from the cave and advances solemnly. On nearing Siegmund she halts. She bears her shield and spear in one hand, rests the other on her horse's neck and remains in this attitude, silently and earnestly observing Siegmund.*)
Siegmund!
Look at me!
I'm—one
you follow soon.

SIEGMUND

(*raising his eyes*)
Who are you, say,
who appear so solemn and fair?

BRÜNNHILDE

The doomed to death
alone may see me.
Who views my form
must part with the light of life.
On the war-plain alone
the valiant see me.
He whom I meet
is chosen for his doom.

SIEGMUND

When you lead on,
whither follows the hero?

BRÜNNHILDE

To Val-father.
You are his choice.
Follow me.
To Valhall we must go.

SIEGMUND

In Valhall does
Val-father live by himself?

BRÜNNHILDE

His noble host
of heroes slain
will throng you round
and give greetings most high.

SIEGMUND

Then shall I find in
Valhall my father Volsa?

BRÜNNHILDE

You'll find your father
the Volsung there.

SIEGMUND

Say, will a woman
greet me with joy?

BRÜNNHILDE

Wish-maids divine
will tend you.
Wotan's daughter too
will proffer you drink.

SIEGMUND

You are high:
I know you as holy
Lord Wotan's child.
Yet one thing tell me, Immortal!
Will brother take with him
his bride who is sister?
Will Siegmund clasp
Sieglinde there?

BRÜNNHILDE

Earthly air
must she keep breathing
Think not to
find Sieglinde there!

SIEGMUND

Then greet for me Valhall,
hail for me Wotan,
hail for me Volsa
and all the heroes—
hail too the fair and
gracious wish-maids.
I will not follow you there.

Das ist Hundings Horn!
Seine Meute naht
mit mächt'ger Wehr:
kein Schwert frommt
vor der Hunde Schwall:
wirf es fort, Siegmund!
Siegmund, wo bist du?
Ha dort! Ich sehe dich!
Schrecklich' Gesicht!
Rüden fletschen
die Zähne nach Fleisch;
sie achten nicht
deines edlen Blicks;
bei den Füssen packt dich
das feste Gebiss —
du fällst —
in Stücken zerstaucht das Schwert.
Die Esche stürzt —
es bricht der Stamm!
Bruder, mein Bruder!
Siegmund — ha!
(*Sie sinkt ohnmächtig in Siegmunds Arme.*)

SIEGMUND
Schwester! Geliebte!
(*Er lauscht ihrem Atem und überzeugt sich, dass sie noch lebt. Er lässt sie an sich herabgleiten, so dass sie, als er sich selbst zum Sitze niederlässt, mit ihrem Haupt auf seinem Schoss zu ruhen kommt. Langes Schweigen, währenddessen Siegmund mit zärtlicher Sorge über Sieglinde sich hinneigt und mit einem langen Kuss ihr die Stirn küsst.*)

(*Brünnhilde, ihr Ross am Zaume geleitend, tritt aus der Höhle und schreitet langsam und feierlich nach vorne. Sie hält in grösserer Nähe an. Sie trägt Schild und Speer in der einen Hand, lehnt sich mit der andern an den Hals des Rosses und betrachtet so mit ernster Miene Siegmund.*)

BRÜNNHILDE
Siegmund!
Sieh auf mich!
Ich bin's,
der bald du folgst.

SIEGMUND
(*richtet den Blick zu ihr auf*)
Wer bist du, sag,
die so schön und ernst mir erscheint?

BRÜNNHILDE
Nur Todgeweihten
taugt mein Anblick;
wer mich erschaut,

der scheidet vom Lebenslicht.
Auf der Walstatt allein
erschein' ich Edlen:
wer mich gewahrt,
zur Wal kor ich ihn mir!

SIEGMUND
Der dir nun folgt,
wohin führst du den Helden?

BRÜNNHILDE
Zu Walvater,
der dich gewählt,
führ' ich dich:
nach Walhall folgst du mir.

SIEGMUND
In Walhalls Saal
Walvater find ich allein?

BRÜNNHILDE
Gefall'ner Helden
hehre Schar
umfängt dich hold
mit hoch-heiligem Gruss.

SIEGMUND
Fänd' ich in Walhall
Wälse, den eig'nen Vater?

BRÜNNHILDE
Den Vater findet
der Wälsung dort.

SIEGMUND
Grüsst mich in Walhall
froh eine Frau?

BRÜNNHILDE
Wunschmädchen
walten dort hehr:
Wotans Tochter
reicht dir traulich den Trank!

SIEGMUND
Hehr bist du,
und heilig gewahr ich
das Wotanskind:
doch eines sag mir, du Ew'ge!
Begleitet den Bruder
die bräutliche Schwester?
Umfängt Siegmund
Sieglinde dort?

BRÜNNHILDE
Erdenluft
muss sie noch atmen:
Sieglinde sieht
Siegmund dort nicht!

SIEGMUND
So grüsse mir Walhall,
grüsse mir Wotan,
grüsse mir Wälse
und alle Helden,
grüss' auch die holden
Wunschesmädchen:
zu ihnen folg ich dir nicht.

BRÜNNHILDE

You've looked on the Valkyrie's
withering glance:
you must follow her now!

SIEGMUND

Where Sieglinde lives
in joy and woe,
there will Siegmund live also.
My looks have not paled,
yet still I see you,
You cannot force me to go!

BRÜNNHILDE

While life is yours
be your own lord.
But then, O fool, death must rule.
I am his herald,
so have come.

SIEGMUND

What hero today
shall lay me low?

BRÜNNHILDE

This day Hunding must win.

SIEGMUND

Bring stronger menace
than Hunding's warfare!
Lurk if you like,
looking for spoil.
Choose this man for your prey:
I think he will fall in the fight.

BRÜNNHILDE
(*shaking her head*)

You, Volsung,
hear what I say!
Such is your coming fate.

SIEGMUND

Look at this sword!
Its might was made
that I might win.
I defy your threats with this blade.

BRÜNNHILDE

He who contrived it
dooms you to death.
He has cast the spell from the sword.

SIEGMUND (*angrily*)

Peace! Alarm not
my slumbering bride!
Woe! Woe; Sweetest of wives!
You saddest among all the faithful!
All the world
rages around you
and I whom alone you did trust,

for whom you defied all the world—
I cannot save,
or give my protection—
for what can I do but betray?
Oh, shame on him
who bestowed the sword,
who makes of my triumph scorn!
If I must perish,
I'll fare not to Valhall,
Hella pleases me more.

BRÜNNHILDE

You think so little of
heavenly rapture.
One poor woman
to you is all,
who, tired and ailing,
feebly reclines in your arms.
Is she all you hold dear?

SIEGMUND

So young and fair
you shine to my eyes:
yet how cold and hard,
seen by my heart.
If you can only
show scorn, then be gone,
you wretched, feelingless maid!
But if you must feed on
this woe of mine,
why then, rejoice if you will.
Let my woe pleasure your envious
    heart.
But of Valhall's brittle raptures,
vaunt no vauntings of them.

BRÜNNHILDE

I know all the pain
that is gnawing your heart;
I feel for the hero's
sacred despair
Siegmund, entrust her to me;
I'll keep her safe in my care!

SIEGMUND

No other than I
is to touch this purest of women;
and if I must die
I shall slay her first as she sleeps!

BRÜNNHILDE

Volsung! Reckless one!
Hear my advice:
entrust me your wife
for the pledge she gladly
received when you gave of your love!

BRÜNNHILDE

Du sahest der Walküre
sehrenden Blick:
mit ihr musst du nun ziehn!

SIEGMUND

Wo Sieglinde lebt
in Lust und Leid,
da will Siegmund auch säumen.
Noch machte dein Blick
nicht mich erbleichen:
vom Bleiben zwingt er mich nie!

BRÜNNHILDE

Solang du lebst,
zwäng' dich wohl nichts:
doch zwingt dich Toren der Tod;
ihn dir zu künden,
kam ich her.

SIEGMUND

Wo wäre der Held,
dem heut' ich fiel'?

BRÜNNHILDE

Hunding fällt dich im Streit.

SIEGMUND

Mit stärkrem drohe
als Hundings Streichen!
Lauerst du hier
lüstern auf Wal,
jenen kiese zum Fang:
ich denk' ihn zu fällen im Kampf!

BRÜNNHILDE

(den Kopf schüttelnd)

Dir, Wälsung,
höre mich wohl:
dir ward das Los gekiest.

SIEGMUND

Kennst du dies Schwert?
Der mir es schuf,
beschied mir Sieg:
deinem Drohen trotz ich mit ihm!

BRÜNNHILDE

Der dir es schuf,
beschied dir jetzt Tod:
seine Tugend nimmt er dem Schwert!

SIEGMUND (heftig)

Schweig' und schrecke
die Schlummernde nicht!
Weh! Weh!
Süssestes Weib,
Du traurigste aller Getreuen!
Gegen dich wütet
in Waffen die Welt:

und ich, dem du einzig vertraut,
für den du ihr einzig getrotzt,
mit meinem Schutz
nicht soll ich dich schirmen,
die Kühne verraten im Kampf?
Ha, Schande ihm,
der das Schwert mir schuf,
beschied er mir Schimpf für Sieg!
Muss ich denn fallen,
nicht fahr ich nach Walhall:
Hella halte mich fest!

BRÜNNHILDE

So wenig achtest du
ewige Wonne?
Alles wär' dir
das arme Weib,
das müd' und harmvoll
matt von dem Schosse dir hängt?
Nichts sonst hieltest du hehr?

SIEGMUND

So jung und schön
erschimmerst du mir:
doch wie kalt und hart
erkennt dich mein Herz!
Kannst du nur höhnen,
so hebe dich fort,
du arge, fühllose Maid!
Doch musst du dich weiden
an meinem Weh,
mein Leiden letze dich denn;
meine Not labe
dein neidvolles Herz:
nur von Walhalls spröden Wonnen
sprich du wahrlich mir nicht!

BRÜNNHILDE

Ich sehe die Not,
die das Herz dir zernagt,
ich fühle des Helden
heiligen Harm —
Siegmund, befiehl mir dein Weib:
mein Schutz umfange sie fest!

SIEGMUND

Kein andrer als ich
soll die Reine lebend berühren:
verfiel' ich dem Tod,
die Betäubte töt' ich zuvor!

BRÜNNHILDE

Wälsung! Rasender!
Hör meinen Rat:
befiehl mir dein Weib
um des Pfandes willen,
das wonnig von dir es empfing.

SIEGMUND

(*drawing his sword*)

This sword—
which a false man once made for a
    true;
this sword—
a coward when facing the foe,
useless when turned on the foe,
is useful when turned on the friend!
(*He holds the sword over Sieglinde.*)
Two lives now
laugh at you here.
Take them, Notung,
envious steel!
Take them at one fell stroke!

BRÜNNHILDE

Forbear, Volsung!
Siegmund shall live—
this is my promise—
and Sieglinde also shall live!
The word is said.
Your fate is altered.
You, Siegmund,
take my blessing and win.
(*A horn is heard in the distance.*)
Hark to the horn!
Now, hero, prepare!
Trust to the sword,
and swing it assured.
Your weapon's as true
as the Valkyr is true in pledge!
Farewell, Siegmund,
hero most blest!
We shall meet once more at the battle!

(*She hastens away, disappearing with
her horse in a ravine. Siegmund follows her with his eyes, seeming
elated. Meanwhile it has grown dark.
Heavy thunderclouds hide the hills,
the ravine and the lofty rocks.
Distant horn-calls continue to be
heard and through the following
scene gradually grow louder.*)

SIEGMUND

(*bending over Sieglinde*)

Slumber's charm
has softly soothed
my fair one's pain and grief.
When the Valkyrie met my path
did she bring this blissful repose?
Should not the carnage of war
have frightened a suffering wife?
Lifeless seems she,
and yet she lives.
The sad one has found
a beautiful dream.

(*new horn-call*)

So slumber right on
till the fight is fought,
and peace has brought you joy.
(*He lays her gently on the rocky seat,
kisses her brow and, after the horns
have been heard again, makes ready
to go.*)
You there who call,
ready yourself.
Soon he shall have
what is due.
Notung knows what to pay!
(*He hastens to the back and disappears
in the black mists on the mountain
peak.*)

SIEGLINDE (*dreaming*)

Father, come back to our home!
He still dwells in the woods
with the boy.
Mother! Mother!
My courage fails!
The strangers seem not
friendly and peaceful.
Clouds of blackness—
fumes that oppress—
fiery flames are
licking our way.
They burn the house!
Come and help me, brother!
Siegmund! Siegmund!
(*A fearful thunderclap following
awakes Sieglinde suddenly.*)
Siegmund! Ah!
(*She stares around her in terror.
Thunderclouds gather and from all
sides are heard approaching horn-
calls.*)

HUNDING'S VOICE

(*from the peak*)

Woe-king! Woe-king!
Stay for the fight!
Or shall my hounds come and stop you?

SIEGMUND'S VOICE

(*heard in the distance from the ravine*)
Where have you hid,
that I may swoop on you?
Stay and let me face you!

SIEGLINDE

(*listening, horror-struck*)

Hunding—Siegmund—
Could I but see them!

HUNDING

Come here, you rascally suitor!
Fricka waits for you here!

SIEGMUND
(*sein Schwert ziehend*)
Dies Schwert,
das dem Treuen ein Trugvoller schuf;
dies Schwert,
das feig' vor dem Feind mich verrät:
frommt es nicht gegen den Feind,
so fromm es denn wider den Freund!
(*Er zückt das Schwert auf Sieglinde.*)
Zwei Leben
lachen dir hier:
nimm sie, Notung,
neidischer Stahl!
Nimm sie mit einem Streich!

BRÜNNHILDE
Halt ein, Wälsung!
Höre mein Wort!
Sieglinde lebe —
und Siegmund lebe mit ihr!
Beschlossen ist's;
das Schlachtlos wend' ich:
dir, Siegmund,
schaff ich Segen und Sieg!
(*Man hört aus dem fernen Hintergrunde Hornrufe erschallen.*)
Hörst du den Ruf?
Nun rüste dich, Held!
Traue dem Schwert
und schwing es getrost:
treu hält dir die Wehr,
wie die Walküre treu dich schützt!
Leb wohl, Siegmund,
seligster Held!
(*Sie stürmt fort und verschwindet mit
dem Ross in einer Seitenschlucht.
Siegmund blickt ihr freudig und er-
hoben nach. Die Bühne hat sich allmählich verfinstert; schwere Gewitterwolken senken sich auf den Hintergrund herab und hüllen die Gebirgs-
wände, die Schlucht und das er-
höhte Bergjoch nach und nach gänzlich ein.*)

SIEGMUND
(*über Sieglinde geneigt*)
Zauberfest
bezähmt ein Schlaf
der Holden Schmerz und Harm.
Da die Walküre zu mir trat,
schuf sie ihr den wonnigen Trost?
Sollte die grimmige Wal
nicht schrecken ein gramvolles Weib?
Leblos scheint sie,
die dennoch lebt:
der Traurigen kost
ein lächelnder Traum.

(*neue Hornrufe*)
So schlummre nun fort,
bis die Schlacht gekämpft
und Friede dich erfreu'!
(*Er legt sie sanft auf den Steinsitz und
küsst ihr zum Abschied die Stirn.
Siegmund vernimmt Hundings Hornruf und bricht entschlossen auf.*)
Der dort mich ruft,
rüste sich nun;
was ihm gebührt,
biet' ich ihm:
Notung zahl' ihm den Zoll!
(*Er eilt dem Hintergrunde zu und
verschwindet, auf dem Joch ange-
kommen, sogleich in finsterem Ge-
wittergewölk.*)

SIEGLINDE (*träumend*)
Kehrte der Vater nur heim!
Mit dem Knaben noch weilt er im
Forst.
Mutter! Mutter!
Mir bangt der Mut:
nicht freund und friedlich
scheinen die Fremden!
Schwarze Dämpfe —
schwüles Gedünst —
feurige Lohe
leckt schon nach uns —
es brennt das Haus —
zu Hilfe, Bruder!
Siegmund! Siegmund!
(*Sie springt auf. Starker Blitz und
Donner.*)
Siegmund! Ha!
(*Sie starrt in Angst um sich her: fort-
während Blitz und Donner. Der
Hornruf Hundings ertönt in der
Nähe.*)

HUNDINGS STIMME
(*vom Bergjoch her*)
Wehwalt! Wehwalt!
Steh mir zum Streit,
sollen dich Hunde nicht halten!

SIEGMUNDS STIMME
(*von weiter hinten her, aus
der Schlucht*)
Wo birgst du dich,
dass ich vorbei dir schoss?
Steh, dass ich dich stelle!

SIEGLINDE
(*in furchtbarer Aufregung lauschend*)
Hunding! Siegmund!
Könnt' ich sie sehen!

HUNDING
Hieher, du frevelnder Freier!
Fricka fälle dich hier!

SIEGMUND

(*now also on the rocky peak*)
You think me still weaponless,
craven rogue!
Threat not with women,
but fight unaided,
else think not Fricka will help!
For see, from the tree that
grows in your house
I drew, undaunted, the sword.

(*A lightning flash, lighting up the crag,
momentarily reveals Hunding and
Siegmund fighting.*)

SIEGLINDE

Stay your hands, you foemen!
Murder me first!

(*She rushes toward the peak, but so
violent a lightning flash breaks that
she staggers back blinded. In the
glare Brünnhilde is seen, soaring over
Siegmund and covering him with her
shield.*)

BRÜNNHILDE

Slay him, Siegmund!
Trust in your sword!

(*Just as Siegmund aims a deadly blow
at Hunding a reddish glow breaks
through the clouds, heralding Wotan,
who stands above Hunding and
points his spear at Siegmund.*)

WOTAN

Get back from the spear!
In pieces the sword!

(*Brünnhilde, with her shield, has re-
coiled in terror. Siegmund's sword
is shivered on the outstretched spear;
Hunding buries his sword in Siegmund's breast. Siegmund falls. Sieglinde, hearing his dying groan, falls
senseless. The glow then vanishes and
the lightning stops. Darkness en-
shrouds the scene. Brünnhilde, dimly
visible, hastens to the assistance of
Sieglinde.*)

BRÜNNHILDE

To horse, that I may save you!

(*She lifts Sieglinde on to the horse
which stands in the defile close by
and immediately disappears with her.
The clouds part in the midst and
show clearly Hunding withdrawing
his sword from the fallen foe. Wotan,
surrounded by clouds, stands behind
him on a rock, leaning on his spear
and gazing sorrowfully on Siegmund's body.*)

WOTAN

Away, knave!
Kneel before Fricka
Tell her that Wotan's spear
avenged what brought her shame.
Go! Go!

(*He makes a contemptuous gesture
with his hand and Hunding falls
dead.*)

But Brünnhilde—
woe to that criminal!
Fearful shall
her punishment be
if once I reach her in flight!

(*He vanishes amid thunder and
lightning.*)

ACT THREE

The Summit of a Rocky Mountain

*To the right, a forest of fir trees. Left,
the entrance to a cave. Above this
the rock rises high. At back the view
is uninterrupted. Rocks of various
sizes form an embankment to the
precipice. Occasional clouds fly past
the summit, storm-swept.*

*Gerhilde, Ortlinde, Waltraute and
Schwertleite, are ensconced on the
rocky peak above the cave. They are
in full armor.*

GERHILDE

(*higher placed than the rest, calls
toward the back*)
Ho-yo-to-ho! Ho-yo-to-ho!
Hi-ya-ha! Hi-ya-ha!
Helmwige, here!
Hie here with your horse!

HELMWIGE'S VOICE

Ho-yo-to-ho! Ho-yo-to-ho!
Hi-ya-ha!

(*A flash of lightning breaks through a
passing cloud: a Valkyrie on horse-
back is visible in it: over her saddle
hangs a slain warrior.*)

GERHILDE, WALTRAUTE & SCHWERTLEITE

Hi-ya-ha! Hi-ya-ha!

(*The cloud with the apparition disappears behind a fir tree on the right.*)

ORTLINDE

(*shouting in the direction of the
fir tree*)
Your stallion should be by
Ortlinde's mare.
My Gray is glad to
graze with your Brownie.

SIEGMUND

Noch wähnst du mich waffenlos,
feiger Wicht?
Drohst du mit Frauen,
so ficht nun selber,
sonst lässt dich Fricka im Stich!
Denn sieh: deines Hauses
heimischem Stamm
entzog ich zaglos das Schwert;
seine Schneide schmecke jetzt du!

SIEGLINDE

Haltet ein, ihr Männer!
Mordet erst mich!

(*Sie stürzt auf das Bergjoch zu:
in dem Lichtglanz erscheint Brünnhilde über Siegmund schwebend und
diesen mit dem Schilde deckend.*)

BRÜNNHILDE

Triff ihn Siegmund!
Traue dem Schwert!

(*Als Siegmund soeben zu einem tödli-
chen Streich auf Hunding ausholt,
bricht von links her ein glühend röt-
licher Schein durch das Gewölk aus,
in welchem Wotan erscheint, über
Hunding stehend und seinen Speer
Siegmund quer entgegenhaltend.*)

WOTAN

Zurück vor dem Speer!
In Stücken das Schwert!

(*Brünnhilde weicht erschrocken vor
Wotan mit dem Schilde zurück:
Siegmunds Schwert zerspringt an
dem vorgehaltenen Speer. Dem Un-
bewehrten stösst Hunding seinen
Speer in die Brust. Siegmund stürzt
tot zu Boden. Sieglinde, die seinen
Todesseufzer gehört, sinkt mit einem
Schrei wie leblos zusammen. Brünnhilde wird undeutlich sichtbar, wie
sie in jäher Hast sich Sieglinde
zuwendet.*)

BRÜNNHILDE

Zu Ross, dass ich dich rette!

(*Sie hebt Sieglinde schnell zu sich auf
ihr Ross, und verschwindet sogleich
mit ihr. Alsbald zerteilt sich das Gewölk in der Mitte, so dass man
deutlich Hunding gewahrt, der
soeben seinen Speer dem gefallenen
Siegmund aus der Brust zieht.
Wotan steht dahinter auf einem
Felsen schmerzlich auf Siegmunds
Leiche blickend.*)

WOTAN

Geh hin, Knecht!
Knie vor Fricka:
meld' ihr, dass Wotans Speer
gerächt, was Spott ihr schuf.
Geh! Geh!
(*Vor seinem verächtlichen Handwink
sinkt Hunding tot zu Boden.*)
Doch Brünnhilde!
Weh' der Verbrecherin!
Furchtbar sei
die Freche gestraft,
erreicht mein Ross ihre Flucht!
(*Er verschwindet mit Blitz und
Donner.*)

DRITTER AUFZUG

Auf dem Gipfel eines Felsenberges

*Rechts begrenzt ein Tannenwald die
Szene. Links der Eingang einer Fels-
höhle: darüber steigt der Fels zu
seiner höchsten Spitze auf. Nach
hinten ist die Aussicht gänzlich frei;
höhere und niedere Felssteine bilden
den Rand vor dem Abhang. Ein-
zelne Wolkenzüge jagen, wie vom
Sturm getrieben, am Felsensaum
vorbei.
Gerhilde, Ortlinde, Waltraute und
Schwertleite haben sich auf der Felsspitze, an und über der Höhle, gelagert, sie sind in voller Waffenrüstung.*

GERHILDE

(*zuhöchst gelagert und dem
Hintergrunde zurufend*)

Hojotoho! Hojotoho!
Heiaha! Heiaha!
Helmwige! Hier!
Hierher mit dem Ross!

HELMWIGES STIMME

Hojotoho! Hojotoho!
Heiaha!
(*In dem Gewölk bricht Blitzesglanz
aus; eine Walküre zu Ross wird in
ihm sichtbar: über ihrem Sattel
hängt ein erschlagener Krieger.*)

GERHILDE, WALTRAUTE UND SCHWERTLEITE

Heiaha! Heiaha!
(*Die Wolke mit der Erscheinung ist
rechts hinter dem Tann verschwunden.*)

ORTLINDE

(*in den Tann hineinrufend*)

Zu Ortlindes Stute
stell' deinen Hengst:
mit meiner Grauen
grast gern dein Brauner!

WALTRAUTE
Who hangs from your saddle?

HELMWIGE
(*stepping from the fir trees*)
Sintolt the Hegeling!

SCHWERTLEITE
Lead off your Brownie
far from my gray one.
Ortlinde's mare now
bears Wittig, the Irming!

GERHILDE
As foemen I saw just
Sintolt and Wittig.

ORTLINDE
(*darting over to the fir tree*)
Hi-ya-ha! Hi-ya-ha! Your horse
is butting my mare!

SCHWERTLEITE & GERHILDE
(*laughing*)
The warriors' strife
makes foes of the horses.

HELMWIGE
(*into the trees*)
Quiet, Brownie!
Peaceful does it!

WALTRAUTE
(*who has taken the place of Gerhilde
at the top of the peak*)
Ho-yo-ho! Ho-yo-ho!
Siegrune, here!
Where were you so long?
(*Siegrune rides by in the direction of
the fir tree.*)

SIEGRUNE'S VOICE
Work to do!
Are the others all here?

SCHWERTLEITE, WALTRAUTE & GERHILDE
Ho-yo-to-ho! Ho-yo-to-ho!
Hi-ya-ha!
(*Siegrune disappears behind the firs.
Two voices are heard from the
depths.*)

GRIMGERDE & ROSSWEISSE
Ho-yo-to-ho! Ho-yo-to-ho!
Hi-ya-ha! Hi-ya-ha!

WALTRAUTE
Rossweisse and Grimgerde!

GERHILDE
They ride as a pair.
(*Grimgerde and Rossweisse, on horse-
back, appear in a glowing thunder-
cloud which ascends from the depths
and vanishes behind the fir tree. Each
carries a slain warrior at her saddle-
bow.*)

ORTLINDE, HELMWIGE & SIEGRUNE
Hello, you travelers!
Rossweisse and Grimgerde!

ALL THE OTHER VALKYRIES
Ho-yo-to-ho! Ho-yo-to-ho!
Hi-ya-ha! Hi-ya-ha!

GERHILDE
Your steeds to the forest
for feed and rest!

ORTLINDE
Tether the mares
away from each other,
until our heroes'
hate is allayed!

HELMWIGE
(*amid the laughter of her companions*)
The gray has paid
for wrath of the heroes!

ROSSWEISSE & GRIMGERDE
(*issuing from the fir trees*)
Ho-yo-to-ho! Ho-yo-to-ho!

THE VALKYRIES
Valkyries, you're welcome!

SCHWERTLEITE
Did you come as a pair?

GRIMGERDE
We rode singly first,
encountered today.

ROSSWEISSE
If we all are assembled,
let's wait no longer:
to Valhall let us be off,
bringing the slain to our lord.

HELMWIGE
Eight are we here,
one we still lack.

GERHILDE
Brünnhilde still is waiting,
tending the Volsung.

WALTRAUTE

Wer hängt dir im Sattel?

HELMWIGE
(*aus dem Tann auftretend*)

Sintolt, der Hegeling!

SCHWERTLEITE

Führ' deinen Braunen
fort von der Grauen:
Ortlindes Mähre
trägt Wittig, den Irming!

GERHILDE

Als Feinde nur sah ich
Sintolt und Wittig!

ORTLINDE
(*springt auf*)

Heiaha! Die Stute
stösst mir der Hengst!
(*Sie läuft in den Tann.*)

SCHWERLEITE UND GERHILDE
(*laut auflachend*)

Der Recken Zwist
entzweit noch die Rosse!

HELMWIGE
(*in den Tann zurückrufend*)

Ruhig, Brauner!
Brich nicht den Frieden.

WALTRAUTE
(*aus der Höhe, wo sie für Gerhilde die
Wacht übernommen*)

Hoioho! Hoioho!
Siegrune, hier!
Wo säumst du so lang?

SIEGRUNES STIMME
(*von der rechten Seite des
Hintergrundes her*)

Arbeit gab's!
Sind die andren schon da?

**SCHWERTLEITE, WALTRAUTE
UND GERHILDE**

Hojotoho! Hojotoho!
Heiaha!
(*Ihre Gebärden, sowie ein heller Glanz
hinter dem Tann zeigen an, dass
soeben Siegrune dort angelangt ist.
Aus der Tiefe hört man zwei Stim-
men zugleich.*)

GRIMGERDE UND ROSSWEISSE

Hojotoho! Hojotoho!
Heiaha!

WALTRAUTE

Grimgerd' und Rossweisse!

GERHILDE

Sie reiten zu zwei.
(*In einem blitzerglänzenden Wolken-
zug, der von links her vorbeizieht,
erscheinen Grimgerde und Rossweisse, ebenfalls auf Rossen, jede
einen Erschlagenen im Sattel führ-
end.*)

**HELMWIGE, ORTLINDE
UND SIEGRUNE**

Gegrüsst, ihr Reisige!
Rossweiss' und Grimgerde!

DIE ANDEREN WALKÜREN

Hojotoho! Hojotoho!
Heiaha! Heiaha!

GERHILDE

In' Wald mit den Rossen
zu Rast und Weid'!

ORTLINDE

Führet die Mähren
fern voneinander,
bis unsrer Helden
Hass sich gelegt!

HELMWIGE
(*während die anderen lachen*)

Der Helden Grimm
büsste schon die Graue!

ROSSWEISSE UND GRIMGERDE
(*aus dem Tann tretend*)

Hojotoho! Hojotoho!

DIE ANDEREN WALKÜREN

Willkommen! Willkommen!

SCHWERTLEITE

Wart ihr Kühnen zu zwei?

GRIMGERDE

Getrennt ritten wir
und trafen uns heut'.

ROSSWEISSE

Sind wir alle versammelt,
so säumt nicht lange:
nach Walhall brechen wir auf,
Wotan zu bringen die Wal.

HELMWIGE

Acht sind wir erst:
eine noch fehlt.

GERHILDE

Bei dem braunen Wälsung
weilt wohl noch Brünnhild'.

WALTRAUTE

Then we must tarry
here till she comes.
Father would give us
greeting most grim,
should he not see her with us.

SIEGRUNE

(*from the rocky peak where she
is looking out*)
Ho-yo-to-ho! Ho-yo-to-ho!
Look here! Look here!
She's coming here now
in galloping haste!

THE VALKYRIES

(*hurrying toward the summit*)
Hi-ya-ha! Ho-yo-to-ho! Ho-yo-to-ho!
Brünnhilde! Hi!

WALTRAUTE

With her tired horse see
her head for the pines.

GRIMGERDE

The fast journey
makes Grane snort!

ROSSWEISSE

No Valkyr before
ever so galloped!

ORTLINDE

What lies on her saddle?

HELMWIGE

That is no man!

SIEGRUNE

It's a maid, truly.

GERHILDE

Then where was she found?

SCHWERTLEITE

She quite refrains
greeting her sisters.

WALTRAUTE

Hi-ya-ha! Brünnhilde!
Can you not hear?

ORTLINDE

Help our sister
off from the saddle!

THE VALKYRIES

Ho-yo-to-ho! Ho-yo-to-ho!
Hi-ya-ha! Hi-ya-ha!
(*Gerhilde and Helmwige head for the
fir trees. Siegrune and Waltraute
follow the two others.*)

WALTRAUTE

But Grane the stalwart has fallen.

GRIMGERDE

See her lift the maid
from saddle to earth.

THE OTHER VALKYRIES

Sister. Sister!
What has occurred?
(*They all re-enter. With them comes
Brünnhilde supporting and leading
Sieglinde.*)

BRÜNNHILDE

Shield me, and help,
my need is dire!

THE VALKYRIES

From whence do you ride
in furious haste?
So gallop those who must flee!

BRÜNNHILDE

I flee for the first time,
and am pursued!
Lord-father dogs my heels!

THE VALKYRIES

Have you your senses?
Speak to us!
What?
Does father follow you?
Why do you flee?

BRÜNNHILDE

O, sisters, look
from the rocky summit.
Look out northward,
to see if he comes.
(*Ortlinde and Waltraute spring up to
watch from the peak.*)
Quick! What do you see?

ORTLINDE

A thunderstorm
nears from northward.

WALTRAUTE

Gathering clouds
congregate there.

THE VALKYRIES

War-father's riding
his heavenly steed!

BRÜNNHILDE

The wild pursuer
draws near from the north!
He nears, he rides and rages!
Shield me, sisters!
Keep her from harm!

WALTRAUTE
Auf sie noch harren
müssen wir hier:
Walvater gäb' uns
grimmigen Gruss,
säh' ohne sie er uns nah'n!

SIEGRUNE
(auf der Felswarte, von wo sie
hinausspäht)
Hojotoho! Hojotoho!
Hieher! Hieher!
In brünstigem Ritt
jagt Brünnhilde her.

DIE WALKÜREN
(alle eilen auf die Warte)
Hojotoho! Hojotoho!
Brünnhilde! hei!

WALTRAUTE
Nach dem Tann lenkt sie
das taumelnde Ross.

GRIMGERDE
Wie schnaubt Grane
vom schnellen Ritt!

ROSSWEISSE
So jach sah ich nie
Walküren jagen!

ORTLINDE
Was hält sie im Sattel?

HELMWIGE
Das ist kein Held!

SIEGRUNE
Eine Frau führt sie.

GERHILDE
Wie fand sie die Frau?

SCHWERTLEITE
Mit keinem Gruss
grüsst sie die Schwestern!

WALTRAUTE
Heiaha! Brünnhilde!
Hörst du uns nicht?

ORTLINDE
Helft der Schwester
vom Ross sich schwingen!

DIE WALKÜREN
Hojotoho! Hojotoho!
Heiaha!
(Gerhilde und Helmwige stürzen in den
Tann. Siegrune und Rossweisse
laufen ihnen nach.)

WALTRAUTE
Zugrunde stürzt Grane, der Starke!

GRIMGERDE
Aus dem Sattel hebt sie
hastig das Weib!

DIE ANDEREN WALKÜREN
Schwester! Schwester!
Was ist gescheh'n?
(Alle Walküren kehren auf die Bühne
zurück; mit ihnen kommt Brünn-
hilde, Sieglinde unterstützend und
hereingeleitend.)

BRÜNNHILDE
Schützt mich und helft
in höchster Not!

DIE WALKÜREN
Wo rittest du her
in rasender Hast?
So fliegt nur, wer auf der Flucht!

BRÜNNHILDE
Zum erstenmal flieh' ich
und bin verfolgt:
Heervater hetzt mir nach!

DIE WALKÜREN
Bist du von Sinnen?
Sprich! Sage uns!
Verfolgt dich Heervater?
Flieh'st du vor ihm?

BRÜNNHILDE
O Schwestern, späht
von des Felsens Spitze!
Schaut nach Norden,
ob Walvater naht!
(Ortlinde und Waltraute springen auf
die Felsenspitze zur Warte.)
Schnell! Seht ihr ihn schon?

ORTLINDE
Gewittersturm
naht von Norden.

WALTRAUTE
Starkes Gewölk
staut sich dort auf!

DIE WALKÜREN
Heervater reitet
sein heiliges Ross!

BRÜNNHILDE
Der wilde Jäger,
der wütend mich jagt,
er naht, er naht von Norden!
Schützt mich, Schwestern!
Wahret dies Weib!

THE VALKYRIES

What's wrong with the woman?

BRÜNNHILDE

Hark to me quickly!
Sieglinde is she,
Siegmund's sister and bride.
Wotan is raging
against the Volsungen pair.
He told me to withdraw
from the brother
victory in strife.
But with my shield
I kept him from harm,
braving the god,
who struck him himself with his spear.
Siegmund fell.
But I flew
far with the bride,
and to save her
hastened to you,
if your fears would let
you hide her from the punishing blow.

THE VALKYRIES

O, foolish sister!
What have you done?
Sorrow! Sorrow!
Brünnhilde, sorrow!
Did disobedient
Brünnhilde
break father's holy command?

WALTRAUTE

(from the height)

Night is drawing
quite near from the north.

ORTLINDE

Heading hither
rages the storm.

THE VALKYRIES

Wild neighs come
from father's steed!
Hear it snorting this way!

BRÜNNHILDE

Woe to this sufferer
when Wotan arrives,
to all of the Volsungs
threatening destruction.
Who's here that will lend
her fleetest of steeds,
to help the woman escape?

SIEGRUNE

Would you have us
rashly rebel?

BRÜNNHILDE

Rossweisse, sister,
let me have your courser!

ROSSWEISSE

The fleet one has never
fled from our lord.

BRÜNNHILDE

Helmwige, listen!

HELMWIGE

I listen to father.

BRÜNNHILDE

Grimgerde! Gerhilde!
Lend me your horse!
Schwertleite! Siegrune!
See my distress!
Be true to me,
as I have been true.
Rescue this woman of woe!

SIEGLINDE

(who till now has stared darkly into
    space, starts up as Brünnhilde puts
    her arm about her protectingly)

Oh suffer no sorrow for me:
death is all that I want!
Who bade you, maid,
to lead me from danger?
Much better had I
received the stroke
from the very weapon
that felled my love.
That way I would have
been one with him.
Far from Siegmund—
Siegmund, from you!
O, cover me, Death,
from remembrance!
Is not my flight
good reason to curse you?
So I beg you, hark to my prayer—
bury your sword in my heart.

BRÜNNHILDE

Woman, live on,
just as love would have you.
Rescue the pledge
you received from his love:
a Volsung grows in your womb.

SIEGLINDE

(gives a violent start, then suddenly
    her face beams with a sublime joy)

Rescue me, brave one!
Rescue my child!
Shield me, you maidens,
with mightiest shield!

(Terrible thunderclaps are heard in
    the distance, then they grow louder.)

DIE WALKÜREN
Was ist mit dem Weibe?

BRÜNNHILDE
Hört mich in Eile:
Sieglinde ist es,
Siegmunds Schwester und Braut:
gegen die Wälsungen
wütet Wotan in Grimm;
dem Bruder sollte
Brünnhilde heut'
entziehen den Sieg;
doch Siegmund schütz' ich
mit meinem Schild,
trotzend dem Gott;
der traf ihn da selbst mit dem Speer:
Siegmund fiel;
doch ich floh
fern mit der Frau;
sie zu retten,
eilt' ich zu euch,
ob mich Bange auch
ihr berget vor dem strafenden Streich!

DIE WALKÜREN
Betörte Schwester,
was tatest du?
Wehe! Brünnhilde, wehe!
Brach, ungehorsam,
Brünnhilde
Heervaters heilig' Gebot?

WALTRAUTE (von der Warte)
Nächtig zieht es
von Norden heran.

ORTLINDE
Wütend steuert
hieher der Sturm.

DIE WALKÜREN
Wild wiehert Walvaters Ross.
Schrecklich schnaubt es daher!

BRÜNNHILDE
Wehe der Armen,
wenn Wotan sie trifft:
den Wälsungen allen
droht er Verderben!
Wer leiht mir von euch
das leichteste Ross,
das flink die Frau ihm entführ'?

SIEGRUNE
Auch uns rätst du
rasenden Trotz?

BRÜNNHILDE
Rossweisse, Schwester,
leih mir deinen Renner!
ROSSWEISSE
Vor Walvater floh
der fliegende nie.
BRÜNNHILDE
Helmwige, höre!
HELMWIGE
Dem Vater gehorch' ich.
BRÜNNHILDE
Grimgerde! Gerhilde!
Gönnt mir eu'r Ross!
Schwertleite! Siegrune!
Seht meine Angst!
Oh, seid mir treu,
wie traut ich euch war:
rettet dies traurige Weib!
SIEGLINDE
(die bisher finster vor sich hingestarrt,
    fährt, als Brünnhilde sie lebhaft —
    wie zum Schutze — umfasst, mit
    einer abwehrenden Gebärde auf)
Nicht sehre dich Sorge um mich:
einzig taugt mir der Tod!
Wer hiess, dich, Maid,
dem Harst mich entführen?
Im Sturm dort hätt' ich
den Streich empfah'n
von derselben Waffe,
der Siegmund fiel:
das Ende fand ich
vereint mit ihm!
Fern von Siegmund —
Siegmund, von dir!
O deckte mich Tod,
dass ich's denke!
Soll um die Flucht
dir, Maid, ich nicht fluchen,
so erhöre heilig mein Flehen:
stosse dein Schwert mir ins Herz!
BRÜNNHILDE
Lebe, o Weib,
um der Liebe willen!
Rette das Pfand,
das von ihm du empfingst:
ein Wälsung wächst dir im Schoss!
SIEGLINDE
(erschrickt zunächst heftig; sogleich
    strahlt aber ihr Gesicht in erhabener
    Freude auf)
Rette mich, Kühne!
Rettet mein Kind!
Schirmt mich, ihr Mädchen,
mit mächtigstem Schutz!
(Immer finsterers Gewitter steigt im
    Hintergrund auf: nahender Don-
    ner.)

WALTRAUTE
(*from the height*)
The storm gathers fast.

ORTLINDE
Flee, you who fear it!

THE VALKYRIES
Hence with the woman,
Woe's in her wake.
No Valkyr would dare to
hold her from harm.

SIEGLINDE
(*on her knees before Brünnhilde*)
Rescue me, maid!
Rescue the mother!

BRÜNNHILDE
Then flee with all swiftness,
and flee by yourself.
I'll—stay where I am,
waiting for Wotan's vengeance,
and then bearing
the brunt of his wrath
giving you time to run from his rage.

SIEGLINDE
Where may I safely travel?

BRÜNNHILDE
Which of you, sisters,
knows what lies eastward?

SIEGRUNE
Far hence, due east,
stretches a wood.
The Nibelung hoard
was brought by Fafner therein.

SCHWERTLEITE
There he did turn
into a dragon;
and in a cave he
broods over Alberich's ring.

GRIMGERDE
An uncanny place
for a helpless bride.

BRÜNNHILDE
And yet within those woods
Wotan's wrath cannot reach.
Our mighty father
avoids them with fear.

WALTRAUTE
Wrathful, Wotan
rides to the rock!

THE VALKYRIES
Brünnhilde, hear
how he comes with a roar!

BRÜNNHILDE
(*pointing the way to Sieglinde*)
Off then, quickly,
and head toward the east!
Bold in defiance,
endure every trial,
hunger and thirst,
briers and stones.
Laugh, whether need
or suffering gnaws.
For one thing know,
and know it ever:
the world's most glorious hero
lives, O woman,
and grows in your womb!
(*She takes the pieces of Siegmund's
sword from under her breastplate
and gives them to Sieglinde.*)
Guard well for his sake
these broken pieces.
Where his father perished
I luckily found them.
Who swings this sword
when forged anew
may take the name that I give—
Siegfried the victor shall thrive.

SIEGLINDE
You noblest wonder!
Glorious maid!
My thanks for bringing
holiest balm!
For him whom we loved
I save the beloved.
May my thanks someday
bless and repay!
Fare you well!
Be blest in Sieglinde's woe!
(*She hastens away. The rocky heights
are veiled in black thunderclouds. A
terrible storm is gathering. A lurid
glow appears in the fir trees. Be-
tween peals of thunder Wotan's voice
is heard.*)

WOTAN'S VOICE
Stay! Brünnhilde!

THE VALKYRIES
The rock's been reached by
horse and rider.
Woe! Brünnhilde!
Vengeance has come!

WALTRAUTE (*auf der Warte*)
Der Sturm kommt heran.

ORTLINDE
Flieh', wer ihn fürchtet!

DIE WALKÜREN
Fort mit dem Weibe,
droht ihm Gefahr:
der Walküren keine
wag' ihren Schutz!

SIEGLINDE
(*auf den Knien vor Brünnhilde*)
Rette mich, Maid!
Rette die Mutter!

BRÜNNHILDE
So fliehe denn eilig
und fliehe allein!
Ich bleibe zurück,
biete mich Wotans Rache:
an mir zögr' ich
den Zürnenden hier,
während du seinem Rasen entrinnst.

SIEGLINDE
Wohin soll ich mich wenden?

BRÜNNHILDE
Wer von euch Schwestern
schweifte nach Osten?

SIEGRUNE
Nach Osten weithin
dehnt sich ein Wald:
der Nib'lungen Hort
entführte Fafner dorthin.

SCHWERTLEITE
Wurmesgestalt
schuf sich der Wilde:
in einer Höhle
hütet er Alberichs Reif!

GRIMGERDE
Nicht geheu'r ist's dort
für ein hilflos' Weib.

BRÜNNHILDE
Und doch vor Wotans Wut
schützt sie sicher der Wald:
ihn scheut der Mächt'ge
und meidet den Ort.

WALTRAUTE
Furchtbar fährt
dort Wotan zum Fels.

DIE WALKÜREN
Brünnhilde, hör'
seines Nahens Gebraus!

BRÜNNHILDE
(*Sieglinde die Richtung weisend*)
Fort denn eile,
nach Osten gewandt!
Mutigen Trotzes
ertrag' alle Müh'n,
Hunger und Durst,
Dorn und Gestein;
lache, ob Not,
ob Leiden dich nagt!
Denn eines wiss'
und wahr' es immer:
den hehrsten Helden der Welt
hegst du, o Weib,
im schirmenden Schoss!
(*Sie zieht die Stücke von Siegmunds
Schwert unter ihrem Panzer hervor
und überreicht sie Sieglinde.*)
Verwahr' ihm die starken
Schwertesstücken;
seines Vaters Walstatt
entführt' ich sie glücklich:
der neugefügt
das Schwert einst schwingt,
den Namen nehm er von mir —
"Siegfried" erfreu' sich des Sieg's!

SIEGLINDE
O hehrstes Wunder!
Herrlichste Maid!
Dir Treuen dank ich
heiligen Trost!
Für ihn, den wir liebten,
rett' ich das Liebste:
meines Dankes Lohn
lache dir einst!
Lebe wohl!
Dich segnet Sieglindes Weh!
(*Sie eilt rechts im Vordergrunde von
dannen. Die Felsenhöhe ist von
schwarzen Gewitterwolken umlagert;
furchtbarer Sturm braust aus dem
Hintergrunde daher, wachsender
Feuerschein rechts daselbst.*)

WOTANS STIMME
Steh, Brünnhild'!

DIE WALKÜREN
Den Fels erreichten
Ross und Reiter!
Weh, Brünnhild'!
Rache entbrennt!

BRÜNNHILDE

Ah, sisters, help!
My heart is faint!
His wrath will blast me
unless you shelter me now.

THE VALKYRIES
(*ascending to the top of the peak,*
concealing Brünnhilde)

Come here, you lost one!
Keep out of sight!
Cling quite close to us.
Say nothing when called!
Woe!
Wotan wildly
leaps from his horse—
here he comes,
revenge in his stride!
(*Wotan, in a frenzy, emerges from the*
firs and halts at the foot of the
height on which the Valkyries are
grouped, hiding Brünnhilde.)

WOTAN

Where is Brünnhilde?
Where is the criminal?
Dare you to hide
the guilty from vengeance?

THE VALKYRIES

Loud are your cries of anger!
O father, what have your daughters
done to arouse you
to furious rage?

WOTAN

Must you thus scorn me?
Watch yourselves, vixens!
I know: Brünnhilde's
hiding from me.
Shrink from the maid,
one cast off forever,
who by herself
cast off her worth!

THE VALKYRIES

She came here because followed,
and with tears pleaded for aid,
Fear and trembling
grip the pursued one.
For our fearful sister
humbly we sue,
that you tame the anger you feel.

WOTAN

Weak-spirited,
womanish brood!
Are feeble hearts
the fruit of my loins?
Was this why I made you

zealous for war,
giving you hearts
that are hard and sharp,
just to have you make moans and
    groans
when my anger is turned on a wretch?
So learn then, whimperers,
just what she did,
for which you weaklings
have poured out your tears.
No one as she
knew all my innermost thinking;
No one as she
fathomed the spring of my motives;
herself was
the desire that fashioned my deeds.
And now she tramples
the holiest tie,
and breaks all faith
in despite of my will,
and openly scorns
what I command
and against me threats with the spear
that she bore by Wotan's wish!
Hear me, Brünnhilde?
You, to whom corslet,
helm and arms,
favor and joy,
being and honor were lent!
Hearing the plaint I am raising,
You seem to fear the plaintiff
as coward who flees her fate!

BRÜNNHILDE

(*She comes forward out of the band*
of the Valkyries and moves with
humble but firm steps down the rock
to within a short distance from her
father.)

Here am I, Father:
I ask to be punished.

WOTAN

I—punish you not:
You yourself have punished yourself.
My will alone
awoke you to life,
yet your will was willed against mine.
You were to follow
the orders I gave,
yet have given orders against me.
Wish-maid
you have been,
yet against my wish you have wished.
Shield-maid
you have been,
yet against me lifted your shield.
Lot-chooser you
were to me,

BRÜNNHILDE
Ach, Schwestern, helft!
Mir schwankt das Herz!
Sein Zorn zerschellt mich,
wenn euer Schutz ihn nicht zähmt.

DIE WALKÜREN
(*flüchten ängstlich nach der Felsenspitze hinauf; Brünnhilde lässt sich
von ihnen nachziehen*)
Hieher, Verlorne!
Lass dich nicht seh'n!
Schmiege dich an uns
und schweige dem Ruf!
Weh!
Wütend schwingt sich
Wotan vom Ross!
Hieher rast
sein rächender Schritt!
(*Wotan tritt in höchster zorniger Auf-
geregtheit aus. dem Tann auf und
schreitet vor der Gruppe der Walküren auf der Höhe, nach Brünnhilde spähend, heftig einher.*)

WOTAN
Wo ist Brünnhild',
wo die Verbrecherin?
Wagt ihr, die Böse
vor mir zu bergen?

DIE WALKÜREN
Schrecklich ertost dein Toben!
Was taten, Vater, die Töchter,
dass sie dich reizten
zu rasender Wut?

WOTAN
Wollt ihr mich höhnen?
Hütet euch, Freche!
Ich weiss: Brünnhilde
bergt ihr vor mir.
Weichet von ihr,
der ewig Verworfnen,
wie ihren Wert
von sich sie warf!

DIE WALKÜREN
Zu uns floh die Verfolgte.
Unsern Schutz flehte sie an!
Mit Furcht und Zagen
fasst sie dein Zorn:
für die bange Schwester
bitten wir nun,
dass den ersten Zorn du bezähmst.
Lass dich erweichen füir sie,
zähme deinen Zorn!

WOTAN
Weichherziges
Weibergezücht!
So matten Mut
gewannt ihr von mir?
Erzog ich euch kühn,

zum Kampfe zu zieh'n,
schuf ich die Herzen
euch hart und scharf,
dass ihr Wilden nun weint und greint,
wenn mein Grimm eine Treulose straft?
So wisst denn, Winselnde,
was sie verbrach,
um die euch Zagen
die Zähre entbrennt:
Keine wie sie
kannte mein innerstes Sinnen:
keine wie sie
wusste den Quell meines Willens!
Sie selbst war
meines Wunsches schaffender Schoss:
und so nun brach sie
den seligen Bund,
dass treulos sie
meinem Willen getrotzt,
mein herrschend Gebot
offen verhöhnt,
gegen mich die Waffe gewandt,
die mein Wunsch allein ihr schuf!
Hörst du's, Brünnhilde?
Du, der ich Brünne,
Helm und Wehr,
Wonne und Huld,
Namen und Leben verlieh?
Hörst du mich Klage erheben
und birgst dich bang' dem Kläger,
dass feig' du der Straf' entflöhst?

BRÜNNHILDE
(*tritt aus der Schar der Walküren hervor, schreitet demütigen, doch festen
Schrittes von der Felsenspitze herab
und tritt so in geringer Entfernung
vor Wotan*)
Hier bin ich, Vater:
gebiete die Strafe!

WOTAN
Nicht straf' ich dich erst:
deine Strafe schufst du dir selbst.
Durch meinen Willen
warst du allein:
gegen ihn doch hast du gewollt;
meinen Befehl nur
führtest du aus:
gegen ihn doch hast du befohlen;
Wunschmaid
warst du mir:
gegen mich doch hobst du den Schild;
Loskieserin
warst du mir:
gegen mich doch hast du gewünscht;
Schildmaid
warst du mir:

yet have chosen lots for my downfall.
Hero-carrier
you have been,
yet have stirred up heroes against me.
What once you were,
Wotan has told you.
What now you are,
that tell to yourself!
Wish-maid are you no more;
Valkyrie are you no longer.
So be henceforth
the thing you are now!

BRÜNNHILDE
(*violently agitated*)
Then you cast me off?
Is that what you mean?

WOTAN
No more shall I send you from Valhall,
no more shall you call
heroes to death;
no more bring the victors
to fill my hall.
When the gods enjoy the banquet
no more will you proffer
drink from the horn.
No more shall I kiss
the mouth of my child.
Our heavenly host
knows you no longer.
You are cut off
from the race of the gods.
Our ties are broken today,
and from my presence you're banished
for good.

THE VALKYRIES
Sorrow! Sorrow!
Sister! Ah, sister!

BRÜNNHILDE
Must you take all things
that once you gave?

WOTAN
You must lose all to your lord.
Right here on this rock
punishment starts.
For now you must lie
guardless in sleep.
Whoever happens this way,
and awakes you may take what he finds.

THE VALKYRIES
Call off, O father,
call off the curse!
Shall the maiden pale
and be withered by man?
Ah, bring not on her

this crying shame,
Give ear to us,
terrible god!
As her sisters Brünnhilde's disgrace is
our own.

WOTAN
Have you not heard
what I've decreed?
Your faithless sister
is banished forever from Valhall.
No more with you
will she ride through the air on her
charger.
Her maidenly flower will fade away.
A husband will gain
all her womanly grace.
She'll have as her master
a masterful man.
She'll sit and spin by the hearth,
as a butt and a mock for scorn.
(*Brünnhilde, with a cry, sinks to the
ground. The Valkyries are terrified.*)
Fear you her fate?
Then flee from the lost one!
She's to avoid,
so keep from her far!
If one should venture
lingering near her,
holding with her
and defying my will,
the fool will share in her fate:
I warn those who might be bold!
Up and away!
Keep from this mountain!
Haste away as I bid you,
lest bad luck light on you here!

THE VALKYRIES
(*dispersing with a wild cry*)
Woe! Woe!
(*They are heard riding away at a
furious gallop. The storm gradually
abates, the clouds disperse, evening
twilight and then night fall amid
tranquil weather.*)

BRÜNNHILDE
Is it so shameful,
what I have done,
that my offense should be punished
with such shame?
Is it so sinful,
what I have done,
that you so harshly should punish that
sin?
Is it so frightful,
what I have done,
that my misdeed should deprive me of
grace?

gegen mich doch kiestest du Lose;
Heldenreizerin
warst du mir:
gegen mich doch reiztest du Helden.
Was sonst du warst,
sagte dir Wotan:
was jetzt du bist,
das sage dir selbst!
Wunschmaid bist du nicht mehr;
Walküre bist du gewesen:
nun sei fortan,
was so du noch bist!

BRÜNNHILDE
(heftig erschreckend)
Du verstössest mich?
Versteh' ich den Sinn?

WOTAN
Nicht send ich dich mehr aus Walhall;
nicht weis' ich dir mehr
Helden zur Wal;
nicht führst du mehr Sieger
in meinen Saal:
bei der Götter trautem Mahle
das Trinkhorn nicht reichst
du traulich mir mehr;
nicht kos' ich dir mehr
den kindischen Mund;
von göttlicher Schar
bist du geschieden,
ausgestossen
aus der Ewigen Stamm;
gebrochen ist unser Bund;
aus meinem Angesicht bist du verbannt.

DIE WALKÜREN
Wehe! Weh!
Schwester, ach Schwester!

BRÜNNHILDE
Nimmst du mir alles,
was einst du gabst?

WOTAN
Der dich zwingt, wird dir's entziehn!
Hieher auf den Berg
banne ich dich;
in wehrlosen Schlaf
schliess' ich dich fest:
der Mann dann fange die Maid,
der am Wege sie findet und weckt.

DIE WALKÜREN
Halt ein, o Vater!
halt ein den Fluch!
Soll die Maid verblüh'n
und verbleichen dem Mann?
Hör' unser Fleh'n!
Schrecklicher Gott,
wende von ihr
die schreiende Schmach!

Wie die Schwester träfe uns selber der
Schimpf.

WOTAN
Hörtet ihr nicht,
was ich verhängt?
Aus eurer Schar
ist die treulose Schwester geschieden;
mit euch zu Ross
durch die Lüfte nicht reitet sie länger;
die magdliche Blume
verblüht der Maid;
ein Gatte gewinnt
ihre weibliche Gunst;
dem herrischen Manne
gehorcht sie fortan;
am Herde sitzt sie und spinnt,
aller Spottenden Ziel und Spiel.
(Brünnhilde sinkt mit einem Schrei zu
Boden; die Walküren weichen ent-
setzt mit heftigem Geräusch von ihrer
Seite.)
Schreckt euch ihr Los?
So flieht die Verlorne!
Weichet von ihr
und haltet euch fern!
Wer von euch wagte,
bei ihr zu weilen,
wer mir zum Trotz
zu der Traurigen hielt',
die Törin teilte ihr Los:
das künd' ich der Kühnen an!
Fort jetzt von hier;
meidet den Felsen!
Hurtig jagt mir von hinnen,
sonst erharrt Jammer euch hier!

DIE WALKÜREN
Weh! Weh!
(Sie fahren mit wildem Wehschrei
auseinander und stürzen in hastiger
Flucht in den Tann. Bald legt sich
der Sturm; die Gewitterwolken ver-
ziehen sich allmählich. In der folgenden Szene bricht, bei endlich ruhigem
Wetter, Abenddämmerung ein, der,
am Schlusse, Nacht folgt.)

BRÜNNHILDE
War es so schmählich,
was ich verbrach,
dass mein Verbrechen so schmählich du
strafst?
War es so niedrig,
was ich dir tat,
dass du so tief mir Erniedrigung
schaffst?
War es so ehrlos,
was ich beging,
dass mein Vergeh'n nun die Ehre mir
raubt?

O, speak, father,
look at me frankly.
Silence your rage!
Soften your wrath!
and say to me plain
the guilt so dark
that compels your stubborn despite
thus to cast off your favorite child!

WOTAN

Ask of your deed!
It plainly tells you your guilt.

BRÜNNHILDE

Yet I obeyed
all your command.

WOTAN

But did I say
you should fight for the Volsung?

BRÜNNHILDE

As lord of the war
you gave me that word.

WOTAN

Yet I revoked the
order given amiss.

BRÜNNHILDE

When Fricka had made you
change your intention,
then you were strange to your thinking,
and a foe to yourself.

WOTAN (*bitterly*)

I believe you understand me,
so punished your cunning revolt.
You thought me, though,
craven and fool.
and had I not treason to punish
you would be too slight for my wrath.

BRÜNNHILDE

I'm not too wise, yet
there's one thing I *do* know:
you had love for the Volsung.
I knew of the strife that
rent your mind
and made your heart so forgetful.
You saw a harsh
alternative woe—
a most bitter thought
paining your heart:
that Siegmund should not be shielded.

WOTAN

You knew this was so,
and yet you gave him your aid?

BRÜNNHILDE

With your weal in mind
I held fast to one thing;
while, in thrall to another,
torn in your thoughts,
helpless, you turned from the problem.
She who kept the rear guard
for Wotan in war,
quite clearly witnessed
what you did not—
Siegmund I beheld.
I faced him,
telling his doom,
encountered his eyes,
gave ear to his words.
I perceived the hero's
sacred distress.
Sad were the sounds
of his manly lamentings—
passionate outcries,
fearful distress,
sadness of spirit,
dauntless disdain.
And my eyes observed,
my ears perceived
that which made me tremble at heart,
in holy, wondering fear.
Shy and stunned,
I stood there in shame.
All I could think of,
how I might serve him,
sharing his fate
in victory or downfall.
What was there other
than this I could choose?
Since he had bred
this love within my heart,
this will that held
the Volsung in my heart,
I trusted his heart,
therefore flaunted his word.

WOTAN

You did the deed
that I longed to do by myself,
but which twofold need
would not let me perform.
You thought joys of the heart
were so easy to come by,
when burning woe
put my heart in pain,
when terrible need
begat my wrath,
and provoked my wish,
for the world's dear sake,
to enchain my love in my bosom.
When, turning my anger
against my own self, I
arose wroth from my

O sag, Vater,
Sieh mir ins Auge:
schweige den Zorn,
zähme die Wut
und deute mir hell
die dunkle Schuld,
die mit starrem Trotze dich zwingt,
zu verstossen dein trautestes Kind!

WOTAN
Frag' deine Tat,
sie deutet dir deine Schuld!

BRÜNNHILDE
Deinen Befehl
führte ich aus.

WOTAN
Befahl ich dir,
für den Wälsung zu fechten?

BRÜNNHILDE
So hiessest du mich
als Herrscher der Wal!

WOTAN
Doch meine Weisung
nahm ich wieder zurück!

BRÜNNHILDE
Als Fricka den eig'nen
Sinn dir entfremdet;
da ihrem Sinn du dich fügtest,
warst du selber dir Feind.

WOTAN (bitter)
Dass du mich verstanden, wähnt' ich
und strafte den wissenden Trotz:
doch feig' und dumm
dachtest du mich!
So hätt' ich Verrat nicht zu rächen;
zu gering wärst du meinem Grimm?

BRÜNNHILDE
Nicht weise bin ich,
doch wusst' ich das eine,
dass den Wälsung du liebtest.
Ich wusste den Zwiespalt,
der dich zwang,
dies eine ganz zu vergessen.
Das andre musstest
einzig du seh'n,
Was zu schau'n so herb
schmerzte dein Herz:
dass Siegmund Schutz du versagtest.

WOTAN
Du wusstest es so
und wagtest dennoch den Schutz?

BRÜNNHILDE
Weil für dich im Auge
das eine ich hielt,
dem, im Zwange des andren
schwerzlich entzweit,
ratlos den Rücken du wandtest!
Die im Kampfe Wotan
den Rücken bewacht,
die sah nun das nur,
was du nicht sah'st:
Siegmund musst' ich seh'n.
Tod kündend
trat ich vor ihn,
gewahrte sein Auge,
hörte sein Wort;
ich vernahm des Helden
heilige Not;
tönend erklang mir
des Tapfersten Klage:
freiester Liebe
furchtbares Leid,
traurigsten Mutes
mächtigster Trotz!
Meinem Ohr erscholl,
mein Aug' erschaute,
was tief im Busen das Herz
zu heil'gem Beben mir traf.
Scheu und staunend
stand ich in Scham.
Ihm nur zu dienen
konnt' ich noch denken:
Sieg oder Tod
mit Siegmund zu teilen:
dies nur erkannt' ich
zu kiesen als Los!
Der diese Liebe
mir ins Herz gehaucht,
dem Willen, der
dem Wälsung mich gesellt,
ihm innig vertraut —
trotzt' ich deinem Gebot.

WOTAN
So tatest du.
Was so gern zu tun ich begehrt',
doch was nicht zu tun
die Not zwiefach mich zwang?
So leicht wähntest du
Wonne der Liebe erworben,
wo brennend' Weh
in das Herz mir brach,
wo grässliche Not
den Grimm mir schuf,
einer Welt zuliebe
der Liebe Quell'
im gequälten Herzen zu hemmen?
Wo gegen mich selber
ich sehrend mich wandte,

helpless affliction,
then a most frightful,
urgent desire
impelled me to further my doom
and to bring to an end my woe
with the world I once had created
You joyed in sweet
and blissful delight,
sensing your rapture,
drunken with joy.
You drank down, smiling,
the drink of love—
while I drink of a drink
mixed of misfortune and gall.
Let your frivolous thoughts
guide you hereafter.
At last you are free from me!
Now I must shun you,
No more may I share
with you my secret counsels.
No more we'll ever labor together.
Nor ever while you live
may the god encounter or greet you.

BRÜNNHILDE

What use was the
foolish maid to you,
who, dazed by your counsel,
misunderstands,
for to me, one counsel
alone could make sense—
to love that which you have loved.
Must I then leave you,
and henceforth shun you?
Must you sever
what once was as one,
abandon half of
what is your being—
that once belonged to you only,
O god, forget not that!
You'll not dishonor
what is eternal,
seeking a shame that
involves yourself.
You just injure your honor
making me mock for your scorn.

WOTAN

You gaily followed
the power of love:
follow henceforth
him whom you must love!

BRÜNNHILDE

If I depart from Valhall,
no more with you working and ruling,
obedient henceforth
to man and his might,
then let no craven

braggart come by;
let whoso wins be
a man of worth.

WOTAN

You've cut yourself off from me.
I may not choose him for you.

BRÜNNHILDE

You brought forth a valorous race;
no coward could spring from such
   lineage.
A hero most high—I know it—
will bloom from Volsungen blood.

WOTAN

Speak not of Volsungen blood!
From them I parted,
parting with you.
Their spite was cause of their doom.

BRÜNNHILDE

She who turned from you
rescued their race.
Sieglinde bears
the glorious fruit.
In pain and woe
Such as no wife has suffered,
soon she will bear
what she hides in fear.

WOTAN

Don't seek or expect
help for the bride,
nor for her fruit to come.

BRÜNNHILDE

She's saving the sword
that you made for Siegmund.

WOTAN

And for him broke in pieces too.
Don't strive, O maid,
to stir up my spirit!
But wait for your lot,
be what it will.
I cannot choose it for you!
Yet now I must fare
forth on my way.
I've dallied with you too long.
So I turn from you
as you have from me.
I dare not know
the thing that you wish.
But this must come:
the meed due for crime.

BRÜNNHILDE

What is your intent
that I must suffer?

aus Ohnmachtsschmerzen
schäumend ich aufschoss,
wütender Sehnsucht
sengender Wunsch
den schrecklichen Willen mir schuf,
in den Trümmern der eignen Welt
meine ew'ge Trauer zu enden:
da labte süss
dich selige Lust;
wonniger Rührung
üppigen Rausch
enttrankst du lachend
der Liebe Trank,
als mir göttliche Not
nagende Galle gemischt?
Deinen leichten Sinn
lass dich denn leiten:
von mir sagtest du dich los.
Dich muss ich meiden,
gemeinsam mit dir
nicht darf ich Rat mehr raunen;
getrennt, nicht dürfen
traut wir mehr schaffen:
so weit Leben und Luft,
darf der Gott dir nicht mehr begegnen!

BRÜNNHILDE

Wohl taugte dir nicht
die tör'ge Maid,
die staunend im Rate
nicht dich verstand,
wie mein eigner Rat
nur das eine mir riet:
zu lieben, was du geliebt.
Muss ich denn scheiden
und scheu dich meiden,
musst du spalten,
was einst sich umspannt,
die eig'ne Hälfte
fern von dir halten,
dass sonst sie ganz dir gehörte,
du Gott, vergiss das nicht!
Dein ewig Teil
nicht wirst du entehren,
Schande nicht wollen,
die dich beschimpft:
dich selbst liessest du sinken,
sähst du dem Spott mich zum Spiel!

WOTAN

Du folgtest selig
der Liebe Macht:
folge nun dem,
den du lieben musst!

BRÜNNHILDE

Soll ich aus Walhall scheiden,
nicht mehr mit dir schaffen und
walten,

dem herrischen Manne
gehorchen fortan:
dem feigen Prahler
gib mich nicht preis!
Nicht wertlos sei er,
der mich gewinnt.

WOTAN

Von Walvater schiedest du,
nicht wählen darf er für dich.

BRÜNNHILDE

Du zeugtest ein edles Geschlecht;
kein Zager kann je ihm entschlagen:
der weihlichste Held — ich weiss es —
entblüht dem Wälsungenstamm!

WOTAN

Schweig von dem Wälsungenstamm!
Von dir geschieden,
schied ich von ihm:
vernichten musst' ihn der Neid!

BRÜNNHILDE

Die von dir sich riss,
rettete ihn.
Sieglinde hegt
die heiligste Frucht;
in Schmerz und Leid,
wie kein Weib sie gelitten,
wird sie gebären,
was bang' sie birgt.

WOTAN

Nie suche bei mir
Schutz für die Frau,
noch für ihres Schosses Frucht!

BRÜNNHILDE

Sie wahret das Schwert,
das du Siegmund schufest.

WOTAN

Und das ich in Stücken ihm schlug!
Nicht streb, O Maid,
den Mut mir zu stören;
erwarte dein Los,
wie sich's dir wirft;
nicht kiesen kann ich es dir!
Doch fort muss ich jetzt,
fern mich verzieh'n;
zuviel schon zögert' ich hier;
von der Abwendigen
wend' ich mich ab;
nicht wissen darf ich,
was sie sich wünscht:
die Strafe nur
muss vollstreckt ich sehn!

BRÜNNHILDE

Was hast du erdacht,
dass ich erdulde?

WOTAN

A heavy sleep
must lock your eyes.
He who awakens the maid
may make her wife, in reward.

BRÜNNHILDE

(*falling on her knees*)

Lest fetters of sleep
firmly bind me,
as easy booty
for any coward,
this one boon must you allow me,
which holy anguish implores!
Put frightening horrors
around me while sleeping,
that only one who's
fearless and free
surely may find me,
on this rock.

WOTAN

Too much is wanted,
too great a boon.

BRÜNNHILDE (*clinging to his knees*)

This one thing must
you allow me!
Oh, shatter your child
who now clasps your knees;
destroy the dear one,
and crush her to bits;
let your spear put out
the spark of her life;
but give, cruel one, not
such monstrous disgrace as this!
At your command
let fire be kindled.
Let blazing barriers
girdle the rock
to lick with their tongues
and tear with their teeth
the coward who rashly ventures to
come near to the terrible rock!

WOTAN

(*gazes at her in emotion as he helps her
to rise*)

Farewell, you valiant,
glorious child!
You, of my heart's most
sanctified pride.
Farewell! farewell! farewell!
Now I must leave you,
and no more greet you
with love and affection.
Nevermore shall you
ride out beside me,
nor hand me mead at meal hour.
Now must I lose you,

you, whom I love so!
O, radiant light in my darkness,
so blazing a fire
shall show your bridal
as never has burned for a bride.
Flickering flames
shall girdle the rock;
The terrible fire
will frighten the cowards.
The weak will flee
from Brünnhilde's rock—
yet one alone masters the bride,
one freer than I, the god!

(*Overcome with joy, Brünnhilde throws
herself into his arms.*)

Your bright and glorious eyes,
that I have often caressed,
when lust for war
was paid with kisses,
when heroes' praises
in childish lisp
were sung from loveliest lips—
these most wondrous, radiant eyes,
that lit my way in the storm,
when hopes and longings
had torn my bosom,
when, with a trembling
and wild emotion
I sought sensual pleasures—
I take this last
joy of my life
in this brief and final
farewell kiss!
A luckier man
will joy in your stars.
On me, hapless eternal,
must you close them forever.
For thus turns
the god from his soul,
so kisses your godhood away.

(*He kisses her on both eyes, which at
once close. She sinks gently unconscious back in his arms. He bears her
tenderly to a low mossy bank, shaded
by a great fir tree. Again he gazes on
her features, then closes her helmet
visor. Once more he looks sorrowfully
on her form, which he at last covers
with the Valkyrie's steel shield. Then
he stalks with solemn determination
to the center of the stage and turns
the point of his spear toward a
mighty rock.*)

WOTAN

In festen Schlaf
verschliess ich dich:
wer so die Wehrlose weckt,
dem ward, erwacht, sie zum Weib!

BRÜNNHILDE
(*stürzt auf ihre Knie*)

Soll fesselnder Schlaf
fest mich binden,
dem feigsten Manne
zur leichten Beute:
dies eine musst du erhören,
was heil'ge Angst zu dir fleht!
Die Schlafende schütze
mit scheuchendem Schrecken,
dass nur ein furchtlos
freiester Held
hier auf dem Felsen
einst mich fänd'!

WOTAN

Zuviel begehrst du,
zuviel der Gunst!

BRÜNNHILDE
(*seine Knie umfassend*)

Dies eine
musst du erhören!
Zerknicke dein Kind,
das dein Knie umfasst;
zertritt die Traute,
zertrümmre die Maid,
ihres Leibes Spur
zerstöre dein Speer:
doch gib, Grausamer, nicht
der grässlichsten Schmach sie preis!
Auf dein Gebot
entbrenne ein Feuer;
den Felsen umglühe
lodernde Glut;
es leck' ihre Zung',
es fresse ihr Zahn
den Zagen, der frech sich wagte,
dem freislichen Felsen zu nah'n!

WOTAN
(*überwältigt, wendet sich zu Brünnhilde und erhebt sie von den Knien*)

Leb' wohl, du kühnes,
herrliches Kind!
Du meines Herzens heiligster Stolz!
Leb' wohl! Leb' wohl! Leb' wohl!
(*Sehr leidenschaftlich.*)
Muss ich dich meiden,
und darf nicht minnig
mein Gruss dich mehr grüssen;
sollst du nun nicht mehr
neben mir reiten,
noch Met beim Mahl mir reichen;
muss ich verlieren
dich, die ich liebte,

du lachende Lust meines Auges:
ein bräutliches Feuer
soll dir nun brennen,
wie nie einer Braut es gebrannt!
Flammende Glut
umglühe den Fels;
mit zehrendem Schrecken
scheuch' es den Zagen;
der Feige fliehe
Brünnhildes Fels!
Denn einer nur freie die Braut,
der freier als ich, der Gott!
(*Brünnhilde sinkt, gerührt und
begeistert, an Wotans Brust.*)
Der Augen leuchtendes Paar,
das oft ich lächelnd gekost,
wenn Kampfeslust
ein Kuss dir lohnte,
wenn kindisch lallend
der Helden Lob
von holden Lippen dir floss:
dieser Augen strahlendes Paar,
das oft im Sturm mir geglänzt,
wenn Hoffnungssehnen
das Herz mir sengte,
nach Weltenwonne
mein Wunsch verlangte
aus wild webendem Bangen:
zum letztenmal
letz' es mich heut'
mit des Lebewohles
letztem Kuss!
Dem glücklicher'n Manne
glänze sein Stern:
dem unseligen Ew'gen
muss es scheidend sich schliessen.
(*Er fasst ihr Haupt in beide Hände.*)
Denn so kehrt
der Gott sich dir ab,
so küsst er die Gottheit von dir!
(*Er küsst sie lange auf die Augen. Sie
sinkt mit geschlossenen Augen, sanft
ermattend, in seinen Armen zurück.
Er geleitet sie zart, auf einen nied-
rigen Mooshügel zu liegen, über den
sich eine breitästige Tanne ausstreckt.
Er betrachtet sie und schliesst ihr
den Helm: sein Auge weilt dann auf
der Gestalt der Schlafenden, die er
mit dem grossen Stahlschild der
Walküre ganz zudeckt. Langsam
kehrt er sich ab, mit einem schmerzlichen Blicke wendet er sich noch
einmal um. Dann schreitet er mit
feierlichem Entschluss in die Mitte
der Bühne und kehrt seines Speeres
Spitze gegen einen mächtigen Felss-
tein.*)

Loge, hear!
Hark to me here,
as when first you were found
a fiery flame,
as when first you escaped me,
a wandering fire:
as you were bound,
be so again!
Arise, wavering fire,
surround this rock! Ring it with fire!
Loge! Loge! Arise!

(*At the last invocation he strikes his
spearpoint three times against the
rock, whereupon a flame leaps up. It
quickly grows to a sea of flame,
which Wotan, with a sign of his
spear, directs to encircle the rock.*)

He who has fear
of Wotan's spear-point
shall never step through the fire!

(*He disappears amidst the flames.*)

END OF THE OPERA

Loge, hör!
Lausche hieher!
Wie zuerst ich dich fand,
als feurige Glut,
wie dann einst du mir schwandest,
als schweifende Lohe;
wie ich dich band,
bann ich dich heut!
Herauf, wabernde Lohe,
umlodre mir feurig den Fels!

(*Er stösst mit dem Folgenden dreimal
mit dem Speer auf den Stein.*)

Loge! Loge! Hieher!

(*Dem Stein entfährt ein Feuerstrahl,
der zur allmählich immer helleren
Flammenglut anschwillt. Wotan weist
mit dem Speer gebieterisch dem
Feuermeer den Umkreis des Felsen-
randes zur Strömung an; alsbald
zieht es sich nach dem Hintergrund,
wo es nun fortwährend den Berg-
saum umlodert.*)

Wer meines Speeres
Spitze fürchtet,
durchschreite das Feuer nie!

(*Er verschwindet durch das Feuer.*)

DAS ENDE